Me, the Boy, and The Monster

Cat McGill

Published by Cat McGill, 2019.

ME, THE BOY, AND THE MONSTER

First edition. February 19, 2019.

Written by Cat McGill.

CAT MCGILL

Me, the Boy, and The Monster is a personal, thoughtful, and touching tribute to a family's journey through the world of adoption and trauma. McGill has a background in developmental psychology and uses this to great effect; the theory sections of *MTBTM* are relevant, researched, and related to real-life examples from McGill's own experience with her adopted son. This book goes beyond the tired cliché of 'attachment' however, pulling together relevant strands of many different psychological theories and disciplines, all of which is juxtaposed against heart-wrenching and emotional accounts taken from McGill's own blog, giving the reader a unique and personal insight in to the day to day struggles of her family.

Readers' Club Offer!

A special offer to all readers of 'Me, the Boy, and The Monster'!

If you've enjoyed reading about our family you might like *What's Next for Unicorns?* – a lighthearted and often laugh-out-loud foray in to the developing brain of our little Fairy as she learns to talk. Available for FREE when you sign up to Cat's mailing list.

To claim your FREE ebook visit http://catmcgill.uk/wnfu

'This isn't just a book for people before they adopt; this is also a book for adopters. There were so many things you said that resonated so clearly with my experience. You articulate the concepts beautifully and the personal illustration from your life, so generously included, brings it to life and makes it real.'

—Adoptive parent

'I LOVE IT! It's written in a really easy-to-understand way, without too much jargon, and the technical stuff is explained in a clear way.'

—Adoptive parent

'Your description of The Monster is a real insight into trauma and its effects on the children. I really gained an understanding and even recognised some traits in our 17-month-old. I appreciate the honesty you have included with your examples – letting the reader know what works/doesn't work and that you have to change your approach as the child develops/heals.'

—Adoptive parent

Contents

Introduction

Let me introduce you to the people in my family. There's me – I'm the mum; Husband – he's the dad. There's Fairy – a funny, empathetic 10-year-old, and my daughter by birth. And then there's Tickle. A sweet, funny, and extremely traumatised little boy, who is my 7-year-old son by adoption.

And then, there's 'The Monster'. The Monster lives inside Tickle, and his job is to protect Tickle from danger, at all costs. The Monster makes fairly frequent appearances in our lives, as he is a little oversensitive when it comes to thinking that Tickle is unsafe. The Monster was quite scary for a while, but these days I think of him as something akin to Sully from Monsters Inc., or one of the ones off Monster Munch packets. Big, fluffy, turquoise... a little misguided, very loyal, and doing his best to keep Tickle safe in the only way he knows how.

I should say at this point that the concept of The Monster is in no way a scientific theory; it is not a piece of researched or peer-reviewed academic work, but a metaphor from my own thoughts, used as a way of making sense of things. For my family, it's proved useful to help us start to understand Tickle and his behaviour – particularly for Fairy. She obviously knows very little of Tickle's early life, but using 'The Monster' we have been able to explain about trauma, and the effect it is having on Tickle in a way that's allowed her to separate out Tickle's behaviour from who he is as a person. She can hate The Monster, but still love Tickle, and that has been really important for her. And for me too, if I'm honest. I don't hate The Monster, because I understand why he's there, but there have been many times where it's been beneficial for me to have him separate from Tickle in my mind.

Tickle shouldn't need a 'Monster'. No child should. Children should have parents that keep them safe. Parents who teach them how to react to different situations, how to pick yourself up when you've fallen over, what to do when you feel sad. Children shouldn't need to worry about where their food is coming from, or if someone is going to take it away. Children shouldn't need to worry that adults are going to hurt them. Children should always have someone to rely on, unquestionably, unconditionally. At the very root of everything, it's all about survival.

In some ways, The Monster 'grew' because Tickle didn't have those things. The world is a very big and frightening place, and when you don't have a secure and confident person to help you navigate it, you need *something* to make sense of it all. In this metaphor, The Monster is a part of Tickle – living in the primitive, survival part of Tickle's brain, which we as parents spend time soothing in babies and young children. The Monster has grown out of the part of the brain that makes a baby cry because it's hungry, or needs changing, or wants a cuddle. It's there to help a child survive, to help them connect with the adults around them, to build their place in the world and start to understand how to get their needs met. But for Tickle, part of that equation was missing – the part with the consistent, unconditional, responsive adult. As a result, The Monster was the only thing that Tickle had to help him survive. The Monster grew, and he depended on it. He didn't know any different.

However noble The Monster's intentions are, the fact is it operates on a skewed version of the world as we know it – one where adults aren't reliable, where loud noises can mean danger, and where you don't know if you are safe. The Monster is childish and primitive, his only objective is to keep Tickle safe, and he will do whatever it needs to do in order to achieve this. Sometimes The Monster gets Tickle to run away from things. Sometimes The Monster makes Tickle shout, scream, or talk nonsense at the top of his voice, to drown out the things in his head. Sometimes The Monster hits us, headbutts, bites, kicks, spits, or pushes us – me, Husband, or Fairy.

Our journey with Tickle and his Monster is still very much at the beginning. They've lived with us for nearly two years as I sit writing this, and we are discovering more about both of them every day. I haven't yet worked out all the answers, or discovered the magic wand that will make all our problems go away(!), but I do feel like we have reached a place where we are starting to understand what's going on. That probably doesn't sound particularly momentous to you, but I can assure you, having spent the first year in total chaos, 'starting to understand' feels like an achievement worth marking!

There is a wonderful quote about trauma that I found in one of the many articles I have read since starting the adoption process, and it is this:

> 'This is not about something you think or something you figure out. This is about your body, your organism, having been reset to interpret the world as a terrifying place and yourself as being unsafe. And it has nothing to do with cognition... you can say to people, "You shouldn't feel that way," or, "You're not a bad person," or, "It wasn't your fault." And people say, "I know that, but I feel that it is."' – Bessel Van Der Kolk[1]

For me, that is the essence of The Monster. You can know, logically, that you are safe, but the feelings are still there. The Monster is still there. Our challenge currently is where we go from here.

In those early days, my biggest dream was that with my undying love and commitment Tickle would start to feel as though he's safe and cared for. I suspect this is something a lot of adoptive parents can relate to – the desperate need to heal your child with your love.

I've found the reality to be rather different. After nearly two years I am relying much more on the cognitive understanding than I ever thought I would; trying to find a balance between thinking and feeling, between his emotions and mine, between Tickle's need to hit things and Fairy's need for it not to be her. Love plays a part, but it's only one piece of the puzzle.

I have learned a lot during this time, and if I'm honest, very little of the preparation I did during the adoption process had me ready for what we have faced. This came as quite a shock, as I really thought I was prepared. I already had a child, I'm a qualified teacher, I have worked for years with children with special needs, traumatised and vulnerable children and adults, studied psychology, and read virtually every adoption book I could get my hands on. I can be realistic, and I know that you're never *really* prepared for parenthood in whatever form it takes – but this has gone far beyond the initial shock to the system. This has been an intrinsic lack of understanding regarding the extent of Tickle's trauma, both from ourselves and from the professionals who were supposed to be supporting us, and at times a complete lack of willingness of the professionals to acknowledge it. It has been a fight to get the support services we need in place. I got to a point around 18 months in where I seriously thought I couldn't go on any more.

This book is a mixture of information, and personal reflections taken from my blog, designed to give an insight in to our lives with Tickle, and put all the information into some context. I have tried to mix it up, so you get a theoretical chapter, followed by a chapter giving some personal insights on how understanding the theory has impacted on my parenting. What I'm aiming for is to write the book I would have liked to read – either before becoming Tickle's mother or at the very least soon after we'd met him. I'd like to dedicate it to all the other adopters out there who have children with live-in 'Monsters' – know you are not alone.

From the blog

The walnut under the mountain

I'm drowning.

I'm in bed, at 10.30 on a Saturday morning, because I can't bring myself to get up and face the day. Face him.

On Thursday afternoon, Tickle headbutted me, full in the face. In the nose, actually. It was incredibly painful, and would have been even worse if I hadn't read his body language and reflexively started to move backwards. I suspect a trip to A&E would have been on the cards.

Since the incident, I haven't really spoken to him. Husband and Gran between them have picked up the slack, and I have not had to do much more than say goodnight.

I'm struggling with the idea of being in the same room as him. I was thinking earlier that he doesn't even feel like my son any more, though when I came to write it down I was relieved to find it didn't feel quite right. I do still have that tiny knot, deep in my stomach that connects me to him, though at the moment it feels like a walnut buried under a mountain.

Mostly at the moment he feels like an imposter. An intruder. Someone who has erupted into my life and caused utter chaos, terror, and pain. I know it's not his fault, and usually that's enough to fuel my compassion, my patience. But after 16 months of this, of the never-ending cycle of escalation, a slight unwinding (always temporary) and then ramping back up again, I am worn out.

It feels like it's getting worse, even though it's not really. What I think has happened is that my resilience has stripped away, layer by layer. Every time he hurts me. Every time he hurts Fairy. Every time he shouts at me, bangs his fists on the floor in anger. Throws things. Breaks things. It wears me down.

I know that the best thing to do right now would be to go and play with him, tickle him, make him laugh, replace the difficult memories with happy ones. But I can't. I see his face right in front of mine, looking in to my eyes with anger and hurt. I see the split second before he headbutts me. I feel the months of love I have poured in to his little body, which in that moment mean nothing at all because he only wants to inflict pain. I feel like I am worthless. I am spent.

I broke down on Thursday, big time. Sobbed in to Gran's shoulder. Freaked Tickle out, devastated Fairy. That night when Tickle said goodnight to me, he said 'I hope you feel better soon Mummy and can stop all that crying.'

To this day I don't even quite know whether he understands what happened. He was really struggling to acknowledge the link between what he had done and me crying. I can understand why; the shame, guilt, horror of what he had done was a lot to take in. You could see it on his face; understanding starting to dawn, and then the creeping grin and glazed over eyes which is the sure sign that whatever's in his head is too much to deal with.

I just don't know how much longer I can keep doing this. Disruption is starting to feel more real. It would be horrific, and I don't think any of us would ever get over it, but I simply do not know how much longer I can go on like this.

We have just started therapy. It's our last hope. It's our only hope. That, and the tiny little walnut, buried under the mountain, are the only things keeping me going today.

1 Living with Trauma

Trauma rules so much of our life at the moment, so this seemed like a good place to start. Understanding some of the science behind Tickle's Monster has gone a long way in helping me control my responses to Tickle and manage my own emotions around his behaviours. Not always, obviously – no one likes being headbutted in the face – but understanding Tickle is probably the main thing that keeps me going.

'Trauma' comes from the Greek word literally meaning 'wound', and can be used to describe a myriad of things, including a distressing experience, an emotional shock following a stressful event, or an actual physical injury. It's quite a wide-ranging and non-specific word, which in some ways can be helpful, but at other times is less useful!

In the local authority I live in we have a dedicated team within CAMHS (Child and Adolescent Mental Health Services) for children who have been abused. They've been a great support to us, and have visited Husband and I at home as well as inviting us to their parents' groups and a short course, designed to give parents and family members an introduction to dealing with the trauma that comes with abuse. The course was great, and has shaped a lot of my thinking around how I deal with Tickle's trauma day to day.

One of the first things I learnt on the course is that experiencing trauma doesn't necessarily mean a child is going to have lots of problems. That may sound counterintuitive, but what it means is that the impact of the trauma on the child will depend on lots of other factors; such as the child's level of understanding, their environment, their support network, etc. *There are no rules regarding how trauma will impact a child.*

People may tell you your child should be 'over it' by now; that they are trying to get attention; that 'biological children do that too' (see chapter 9 for my comeback of choice); but just remember this: *there are no rules when it comes to trauma.*

The psychiatrists on the course explained that when they work with a child they are not really interested in whether a child 'should' be traumatised, or 'why' they are traumatised; instead their focus is:

- How an event has affected, or is affecting a child right now
- What barriers are limiting the child's recovery, and what can be done about them
- What resources are available to the child to aid their recovery, and how can these be used effectively

Dr Bessel van der Kolk (considered by many to be the godfather of trauma therapy) says

> 'Trauma treatment is not about telling stories about the past. It's about helping people to be here now. To tolerate what they feel in the present.'[2]

I find this approach straightforward, and cutting to the chase in this fashion really appeals to me. We know what's happened, and we want to move on. What can we do about it? What action can we take? What else do we need to know? It may not immediately suit everyone, but personally I find it quite empowering.

<u>But what's it like to live with trauma?</u>

If you are reading this book because you're thinking about adopting, then you may have spotted already that this book is not always going to be a pleasant read. If you are reading this after having adopted a child, please know you are not alone! It's not always like this, and it can (and does) get better, but I do believe it's important not to shy away from the reality of what it's like to live with a traumatised child.

Here is a piece I wrote for my blog a little while ago, which may give you a picture of what day-to-day life with a traumatised child can be like.

Saturday started at 5.00am, as usual.

Husband took the early shift, also as usual. He seems to need less sleep than I do, and is also blessed with one of those brains that will switch off on demand, meaning he drops off within minutes of getting in to bed.

This particular morning we'd agreed the night before that Husband would definitely get up if it was any early one, as I'd been up early quite a lot of the week and was feeling tired to the point of not quite feeling safe to drive. Needless to say, I then woke up at 4.30, 6.30, and finally at 7.45 – this time by the absolute racket that was coming from downstairs. Quite apart from the noise Tickle was making, Husband is normally very calm and softly-spoken, so the fact I could even hear his voice from upstairs was an indicator that something wasn't right. The fact that his voice was saying 'Tickle, you are not allowed to headbutt me' was an even bigger clue.

Thanks to Facebook messenger, I sent Husband a quick text to say I was awake, and minutes later heard the tell-tale thumping on the stairs.

You really don't need a blow-by-blow account of the next four hours so I shall summarise it thus:

- *Tickle didn't want to talk about his difficult feelings. Instead he tipped over my bin, pulled out my sock drawer, threw a pair of my trousers, and pulled a full bag of clothes that we hadn't got around to putting away from last weekend out of my room and threw it down the stairs*

· Tickle wanted to go to soft play, and was very cross that I wasn't going to take him. He decided to demonstrate his feelings by throwing Duplo blocks at me, down the stairs, and in to the bathroom.

· I decided that I didn't enjoy having things thrown at me, so told Tickle I was going to shut his bedroom door until he'd finished throwing, to keep myself safe. There was lots of screaming, crying, wall-banging, and quite a lot more throwing.

· Tickle opened his bedroom door, and said 'There. I have finished throwing. Now can we go to soft play?' I said no, obviously. He explained that he appreciated my point of view, but thought it only fair to let me know that if I continued to persist with this viewpoint he would have no choice but to throw some more things. (I'm paraphrasing a little.) I said OK. He threw some more things.

· Eventually his bedroom was pretty much completely trashed. His four favourite slide/tunnels were in bits. We had lots of discussions about whether he was ready to tidy up yet, whether we were going to soft play, that sort of thing.

Four and a half hours after the meltdown had started, he was calm, and his room was tidy. We had lunch.

I'd sent Husband out for a run at some point – running off emotions works well for him and he managed to clear out 10k of them that morning. Outwardly, I was still calm, but my inner peace had been somewhat tested during the escapade, and much as I wanted to give Husband an afternoon off I did ask if he felt up to coming out for a walk with Tickle and me. We're trying to get better at self-care, and have realised that when we haven't got much left in the tank we're better off muddling through together, than one person going until they're empty and then tag teaming the other one, who won't have had a chance to recover properly anyway.

So that plan was all fine, until I popped to the loo and Tickle hit the cat. Etta was OK, but Husband had his 'I really can't deal with you today' voice on, so before either of us quite knew what was going on I had whisked downstairs, bundled Tickle in to his coat and had him strapped in to his car seat, with an 'I-will-take-him-no-it's-fine-you're-not-fine-but-I'm-going-back-to-bed-the-minute-I-get-home' thrown over my shoulder.

Tickle and I walked for over two hours. I went through the whole spectrum of emotions during that time; from quietly seething, to snapping at him, to sending passive-aggressive texts to Husband (poor man), to nearly crying when Tickle said out of the blue that he missed his birth mum. I had hoped to put my newly made 'list of people I can call when I need a chat' to good use whilst on the walk, but it's hard to sustain a conversation when you have to keep punctuating it with 'Leave the poo alone', so I didn't bother.

We calmed down. We tired ourselves out. He hit me a couple of times to see whether I'd hit him back, and seemed pretty surprised when I didn't. He tried to eat a stick. We drank hot chocolate, and drove home the long way so we could go over our favourite big bridge.

THOUGH IT MAY NOT SOUND like it, what I've described above was one of Tickle's better meltdowns. Better, in that I didn't get physically hurt, and I felt more or less in control of the situation. This particular day was just after we had started seeing our therapist, and she'd given us a few strategies for looking after ourselves in these situations. (You might have noticed that I left him in his room to trash everything, rather than having stuff thrown at me!)

Fight, Flight, Freeze, Appease

Most people have heard of 'fight or flight', and I think a fair few people will even be familiar with 'fight, flight, or freeze', but I'm not sure I heard of 'appease' until I learned about trauma. These are four common responses to danger, whether real or perceived, and are the brain's way of trying to protect and keep us safe. Before we adopted Tickle, I don't think anyone had ever mentioned them to me in the context of neglect, trauma, and adoption, but I believe they are vital to understand.

I don't think there's necessarily a strictly linear pattern to the responses, but Tickle definitely seems to have worked backwards through them, and from what I understand, freeze and appease are more likely to appear further down the line where neither fight or flight is an option. Bearing that in mind, we can assume that freeze and appease will be fairly common responses for children who've been fostered or adopted – and even more so the older they were when they were taken in to care.

Appease

Before we met him, Tickle was described to us by his foster carer as a 'compliant' child; they seemed quite pleased by this, but it rang loud alarm bells for me. Looking back, I feel so sorry for all of us in those early days – Husband and I were so clueless, Fairy just so delighted to have a brother, and poor Tickle, who was absolutely and utterly terrified. The more I get to know the 'real' Tickle, the more it becomes apparent just how petrified he was when we first met him.

Tickle, like every other child in local authority care, had no choice in what happened to him. He was removed from his parents' house all of a sudden, with no explanation, and taken to a strange house where he was told that two adults he'd never met before are going to look after him. In that situation Tickle had no way of understanding whether he was safe or not, and based on his previous life experiences you could be fairly confident he was going to plump for 'probably not'. After a couple of months living in this house he was then told that he'd got to move to another new house, and – by the way – he's going to get a new mummy and daddy, and a sister into the bargain.

What I hadn't really registered at the time was that Tickle's whole life experience up to that point was that adults hurt you. They don't look after you, they don't meet your needs, they take your food away, they hit and scream at you. Tickle's world was upside down from the one you and I know. It's hard for us to comprehend, but he simply had no frame of reference for believing he was going to be safe.

At this point, Tickle's 'Monster' didn't really know what was going on. There were new grown-ups around, and their reactions were different from the grown-ups The Monster was used to. The Monster wasn't quite sure how to respond to this; caution was advised. The Monster was telling Tickle, 'Until we know the deal, our best bet for staying safe is to go along with it, do what they say, and just hope they don't hurt us.'

For some children, who reach 'appease' after a long period of time with their needs not being met, they have just accepted that this is their lot in life. The safest way to exist is to go along with things.

Some children may stay here for a long time; compliant, careful, always tiptoeing around everyone and trying not to rock the boat. I'm not sure there's an awful lot you can do apart from being consistent and loving. I cannot tell you the number of times Husband and I were racking our brains to think of ways we could convince Tickle that we weren't going to hit him, and all we came up with was 'We'll carry on not hitting him until he believes us'. Tickle has been with us for nearly two years as I write this, and he still asks me almost every day whether I'm going to hit him. (I still haven't.)

The real key thing when thinking about 'appease' is that often the children seem OK from the outside. Take Tickle's foster carer for example – she thought he was genuinely a nice, compliant child. For us, it was the calm before the storm.

Freeze

We have not seen quite as much of the freeze response in Tickle, though he did show us a bit in the early days. It was usually triggered by something in the environment; a sudden loud noise, someone dropping something, or someone raising a hand above their head. When Tickle first came to live with us he didn't cry. If he fell over and hurt himself, he would freeze, his whole body stiffening and shaking, and not making a sound. The first time I saw this happen I was devastated; 'You can cry if you want to,' I said, and he literally collapsed. ('It's OK to cry' has become a mantra in our house.)

Some children may hold their breath. Some children may space out and dissociate completely, internally taking themselves away from their current reality, which is just too much for them to cope with. Tickle used to do this a *lot*, but for him it was combined with his flight response rather than freeze – though it took us a long time to figure out that this was what was going on.

Freeze is quite an obvious fear response – it actually looks like fear from the outside, as opposed to apathy, naughtiness, anger, etc. When Tickle does freeze, or flinch, it's immediately obvious that he's frightened. What has been more difficult for us is when fear simply looks like 'naughty' behaviour.

Flight

Flight doesn't necessarily just mean running away. It can be preparing to run – jiggling legs, restless, attention wandering. In our case, Tickle was running away inside his own head, completely dissociating. We used to call it 'loopy' in the early days, and it was like nothing I have ever seen before. Looking him in the eyes, you could see he just 'wasn't there', it was as if I was looking at a different child. The Monster took *total* control. It would usually start off fairly innocuously – Tickle would start to walk around on his tiptoes, clutching his legs, laughing. His eyes would be wide, and slightly unfocused, and his mouth open and lolling, laughing. Sometimes he would sing 'Happy Birthday' at the top of his voice, as fast as he could, or sometimes he just jabbered nonsense words. Often, he used to run away from us, seemingly with no sense of danger – he had no idea where he was running to, and on one occasion he stepped in to the road in to the path of an oncoming car. These episodes used to terrify me, because the Tickle I was coming to know seemed completely absent. He has perfectly good road sense, for example, and I would happily let him walk along the pavement by himself – in fact he often reminds me not to walk in the road. But if the loopy state hits, there is no telling what he will do. At the best guess, think of whatever you most would like him *not* to do, and that's probably what he'll go for; it's like he's trying his best to create mayhem. To me, it always felt like he was trying to create a feeling of chaos in the real world to match the one inside his head.

Tickle's social worker was supremely unhelpful in these situations, as was CAMHS (worth noting though this wasn't the same department as the one who ran the course I mentioned earlier, this was LD CAMHS, for children with learning disabilities). Tickle's social worker thought he was doing it on purpose, deliberately trying to be naughty, or demand attention. CAMHS came at it from a behaviour-fixing viewpoint and asked whether we had tried a sticker chart. It's really hard to explain to a psychologist that you are not going to follow their advice, because it's not like you have a child who doesn't understand how to behave, it feels more like you have a monster living inside your child's body and sometimes it takes over and creates chaos, simply so your child does not have to deal with whatever fear has been triggered.

(If you find a therapist who understands that principle, then hang on to them and do not let go! In my experience precious few professionals have a proper understanding of trauma.)

Over time we have learned a lot more about these episodes, and have had some amazing insights into them from Tickle himself. Once, he paused, mid-dissociative episode and said, 'I'm trying to calm down, Mummy, but it's difficult.' In that moment, that was the ultimate insight in to what is going on for him. He doesn't want to behave like that; it's frightening and exhausting. He's trying to get The Monster back under control, but it's really bloody difficult. I cannot imagine what it feels like to be so scared that your body just takes over and removes you from the situation. Tickle would often become quite violent during loopy episodes, but afterwards he would appear to have no recollection of what had happened. There have been many times where he's looked at me and asked why I'm so cross, and when I reply, 'Because you just hit me' he will respond with 'Did I?!' as if he wasn't even there. A couple of times he has followed this up with 'How do you know?', which would be hilarious if I was in any mood to laugh at the time!

Fight

There's been child-to-parent violence (known in adoption circles as CPV) in our house for a long time, but originally it came with the dissociated, loopy states, where Tickle didn't know what he was doing. These days it's more likely to come from a place of anger: Tickle doesn't like being told what to do, or not do, or he's frustrated because he can't get his toys to sit the way he wants them to, or he wants breakfast *right now*. He feels like he's got no control over his environment, and that makes him really cross. There have also been a couple of times where I've witnessed an obviously deep-rooted response; once I surprised Tickle from behind, taking his arm, and on instinct he turned his head and bit me. Within a couple of seconds he was looking up at me, horrified, kissing my arm better and saying sorry over and over.

Over time Tickle's meltdowns have definitely mellowed, but in the early days when I was finding things difficult I'd often feel like I was blowing things out of proportion. I might say to a friend 'Tickle pulled Fairy's hair yesterday', and my friend might struggle to see what is so unusual about that. They might have children of their own who often squabble, or they might remember fighting with their siblings as a child. Then I would have to explain to them that Tickle wound both hands in to Fairy's hair and yanked so hard he was practically hanging off her, and she was bent double and screaming with terror.

My friends in the adoption community often share stories about people trying to make us feel better by telling us that 'biological children do that too'. I have an issue with this; adopted children are perfectly capable of having a 'normal' tantrum, but there's another, extra layer, that you will never, ever have to worry about with a biological child. Imagine that someone walks in to your home and your biological child is taken away from you against their will, and against yours. Imagine the panic, the crying and screaming that would erupt from your child. Is that the same as the 'tantrum' they throw when you tell them to turn off the computer and have dinner?

That additional layer of panic that would permeate your biological child's 'tantrum' if someone were forcibly taking them away from you, is the one that adopted children have woven throughout the very fabric of their lives. I remember once Fairy was carrying a plate of stew over to the dining table whilst daydreaming about kittens/unicorns/sleepovers/etc and dropped it all over the kitchen floor – Tickle screamed his head off and had to be held and rocked by Husband, refusing to be comforted until Fairy and I had cleaned up all the mess. I still don't know what exactly set him off, whether it was the noise of the plate dropping or the mess of the stew all over the kitchen – he was screaming, crying, and shouting 'It's disgusting'. I suspect he was terrified at the thought of how we might respond to the incident.

When Fairy, my biological child, has a tantrum, I ask her to go to her room to calm down. I have spent 10 years (so far) teaching her how to deal with her emotions, soothing her when she's sad, and helping her to find a way of regulating herself that works for her. I know that if Fairy goes up to her room then she gets the space she needs to calm down, and I can get on with stuff without a stroppy child in the way. If she makes me so cross that I yell at her, I can take some time out myself, and I can calm down.

When Tickle, my adopted child, has a tantrum, there is nothing I can do but hold him. Tickle cannot regulate his emotions, so it is up to me to do it for him. This means that while he has his 40-minute meltdowns, I am holding him on my lap, rocking him, talking to him in a soothing voice, stroking his hair, kissing his head, and telling him I love him. When he calms down enough that he completes his two minutes of good sitting, I lavish him with praise for how well he's done. We go upstairs together and I get his bath ready, talking to him all the time in a calm voice. I get him in the bath, wash him, tickle him when expected, laugh with him, and play with him.

Many's the night I have sat with tears silently streaming down my cheeks, because giving that much love, peace, and calm to a child who spends 40 minutes hitting you in the face and screaming is draining. Telling a child you love them when they are deliberately farting on you is hard. Stroking and rocking a child who is pulling your hair and spitting on you feels... almost demeaning. He was treating me as if I was nothing. In that moment, I didn't matter. And yet, I couldn't leave him. I had to stay, pouring love in to this little person; pouring in love, and doing my best to take in his anger, fear, and overwhelming sadness so it didn't have to stay inside of him any more.

My God it's hard. It's not his fault. But it is *so hard*.

I do want to pause for a moment, and say that although adopting a traumatised child is incredibly hard, it can also be immensely rewarding. It's easy to get bogged down in the day-to-day struggle, and not remember those amazing moments, like how he now says 'I love you' spontaneously just before he goes to sleep. Like the last time I had a cold and he told me to get in to bed, tucked me in, and gave me a kiss. The first time he put his arms round me for a hug instead of just leaning towards me. The afternoon when we lay belly to belly on the sofa playing that game where he presses my nose and I go 'beep'. The day he came home from school, utterly delighted with himself because he'd learned to write the letter 'p' ('Down, up, and around!'). The time we were sitting round the dinner table and he looked around us all and said 'What a nice family!'. All the times he's thanked me for cooking him such a nice dinner. The pure joy of watching *Frozen* with him and hearing him sing 'Let it Go' at the top of his voice! The first time he was scared of something and ran to me for comfort. When I tell him 'You're my best boy' and he replies with 'You're my best girl'. When he asks me to sing to him at bedtime. Watching him develop from someone who rolls cars down a ramp for six hours a day to someone who puts babies to bed and feeds them, to someone who calls out to his sister 'You be Anna, I'll be Elsa' as they are running to the park. (In the Twitter adoption community, we refer to each of these moments as a #glowmo, and try to make sure we share them regularly, so we don't get too stuck in negativity.)

It's definitely not all bad, and it definitely is a beautiful, wonderful thing to do. But it's something you want to go in to with your eyes wide open, as it is going to be far, far more than you ever imagined.

Trauma and adoption

One thing that really stuck with me from the course I attended at CAMHS was when the psychiatrist was talking about how a child's view of the world changes after a traumatic event. She described it as having their world turned upside down, and our job as helping them get it the right way up again. For all of the other parents in the room this was totally true. They were there because their biological children had experienced traumas. Their children know what 'normal' is like – for them it was like stretching out an elastic band and needing it to ping back into shape. But then the psychiatrist turned to me, and said that some children, if their trauma is experienced very early on in life, can start out with an upside-down world.

In Tickle's world, adults hurt you. They can't be relied upon to look after you, to soothe you when you cry, provide enough food, or even pass the time of day with you. Our job as adopters is somewhat more difficult than that of the other parents who attended that course that day; we have to completely rewrite Tickle's understanding of reality.

Quite a big job.

Two years in, we have been working on this every single day. Even now, Tickle still asks me on an almost daily basis whether I'm going to hurt him, whether Husband or Fairy is going to hurt him, whether Gran is going to hurt him... he's terrified that his birth parent is going to turn up at the house, and we role-play a scenario most nights at bedtime where he asks me what I would say if they did turn up. I say the same thing every day, and the predictability seems to comfort him. It's a mantra we repeat often: 'No one is allowed to hurt Tickle' or sometimes 'In our family, we don't hurt'. This is repeated, multiple times a day, every day, and I'm sure it will be for some years yet.

We have developed various strategies for living with a day-to-day 'Trauma Monster'. But it's a constantly shifting, changing world, and often we suddenly realise that old favourites that have stood us well for months are now making things worse. In the upcoming chapters I'm going to outline things that have worked for us at different times, in the hope that you might find something in there you haven't yet tried(!) or that it at least provides the jumpstart for you to think about something slightly differently.

However, before we get on to that, there's a chapter on self-care. Some people who read early versions of this book told me that they were tempted to skip this chapter, but I can tell you now, I firmly believe this is the single most important chapter in the whole book. If you get self-care right, it is the bedrock from which to build a strong and resilient family. Get it wrong, and it could finish you off. Take it from me, as someone who learnt this the hard way – you don't want to take this lightly.

From the blog

10 things I wish I'd known

1. *Be prepared to take* at least *a year off work. Seriously. No really. Trust me.*

2. Adoption is a hugely emotional journey, and each stage more so than the last. The run up to approval can be harrowing, the wait during matching is unbearable, and then actually having a child placed with you is like living with a small dementor who feeds off your energy. (Love him, obviously, but still...)

3. Read (1) again, and then (2) again, until you believe (1). My biggest regret is pressuring myself to go back to work too soon, even though I am freelance and hardly do any actual work at all. Some days even daytime TV is too demanding for my poor addled brain.

4. Love for birth children and love for adopted children feels pretty much the same. The only difference is that there is a gaping chasm of experiences that Tickle has had which I haven't been involved in, and that can be difficult sometimes. It can be difficult because I want to help him cope with life better, and I feel sad that he's had these experiences, and it can be difficult because sometimes you are basically scrabbling around in the dark to try and work out what on earth is wrong with him.

5. Read books like The Boy Who was Raised as a Dog *and really try to understand that you could end up with a child who has had experiences like these. And then try to understand that you will be completely unprepared for it, regardless of how many books you have read. It's really, really hard.*

6. Get a counsellor, right at the start. I wish I had done this; just having someone impartial to talk things over with and help me deal with all of my feelings would have been such a help. My Husband is great, my Mum is great, my friends are great, but the absolute enormity of what Tickle is dealing with, and therefore what I am dealing with, is far too much to bear without having some sort of outlet. Understand that secondary trauma is a thing and this is why all *counsellors have counselling themselves, only they call it 'supervision'. Supervision for adoptive parents really ought to be a thing.*

7. Get connected to a community of adopters. Twitter is great for this, but I wish I had someone in real life who 'gets' it without me having to explain. I have met people who have adopted a couple of times – just by chance – and nearly cried with relief just to find someone else who knows what it's like.

8. Spend time around children who have special needs. I have worked with music and SEN for years, and it was still a huge leap from that to being the parent of a child with SEN. Even if you're not planning to adopt a child with special needs (I wasn't) still do it.

9. No matter what your child does, there will be someone who says 'Oh, all children do that!'. They are wrong.

10. Everybody brings their own emotional baggage to adoption. Adopters, children, foster carers, social workers, IROs, teachers, grandparents... and as the parent you will be the one in the middle fielding all of it. Self-care is so important. Sometimes you just need to do what needs doing so you can get through, and then give yourself some time to recover. People who aren't adoptive parents don't understand what it's like to be adoptive parents. Stick to your guns, know yourself, stand up for yourself and your family, and follow your gut instinct. At the end of the day, when the adoption order has gone through and all the support and scaffolding drifts away, that is what you are going to be left with.

2 Self-care

All the books I have read that mention self-care all agree it's a fabulous idea. And yet somehow, the chapter on self-care is always stuck right at the back. That is scarily indicative of how we often treat the subject, particularly in relation to ourselves and our own mental health. I'm going to buck the trend here, as I have recently learned that self-care is not only a fabulous idea, it is *absolutely key* to your survival as a healthy human being.

Adopting a traumatised child has been the single most exhausting thing I have ever done. I have dug deep, tapped wells of energy I didn't even know I had, and drained them all dry. Up until quite recently I treated self-care as a lovely add-on. I would try and make sure I had a massage every couple of months (didn't happen). Husband and I would make quality time to spend together (we went to the cinema once). People were frequently asking me 'What are you doing for yourself, though?' And I would wail and grumble that how on earth was I supposed to find the time to do anything for myself when every waking moment I had one child or the other crawling over me demanding attention?

I thought they were being unrealistic. Nice idea in theory, but totally impossible to put in to practice. If you are reading this thinking the same, I urge you to pay very careful attention to this chapter. I am going to be brutal; I will hold nothing back. You need to hear this, because in fact, those people saw something that I was refusing to see. Self-care is *the key*. It is not optional, it is essential, and should be the bedrock of your very existence.

Let me tell you what happened.

On 25 April, I posted this on my blog:

'I have been sat here with this browser window open for at least an hour without writing anything. I don't really know where to start.

I am living in a world of domestic violence. There is not a day that goes past at the moment where someone in our family doesn't get hit, headbutted, bitten, or kicked. Fairy is getting hit on the head about once a week, and only last week had her hair pulled so hard she was pulled right over. Missiles are thrown, sometimes just in a fit of anger, sometime aimed with precision. It's only a matter of time before one of us ends up visiting A&E.

If it was Husband acting like this, the authorities would be all over us. But at the moment war is being raged on our house by a small boy of seven.

It might sound silly, written like that. How can a child do that much damage? And yet Fairy had a lump on her head for a fortnight from something that he threw at her, and the only reason I avoided a broken nose was because I saw the headbutt coming just in time to move back.

We are so worn down. Our resilience has been stripped away, layer by layer. I have been trying to work out recently why it feels to us like things are so much worse, but when we look at it objectively, actually they're not. I mean, they are worse, but not by the amount it often feels like. Maybe my perspective has skewed completely; a good day now is one where he's only hit someone once, and at least it's a family member and not a total stranger. Or maybe we simply have nothing left to give.

Husband and I were wondering this morning whether it would feel different if we didn't have the 'giving him back' option looming over us. Would I feel better if I just accepted that we are committed to Tickle, and that we will go ahead with the adoption order regardless? Are we torturing ourselves unnecessarily by giving ourselves a choice in the matter?

It's horrible to admit that disruption is actually on the cards for us. I can't even begin to describe how it feels to be seriously considering asking social services to take my son away, especially knowing the impact that is going to have on his life. It's more than just moving on to another family; he wouldn't be adopted now, so he'd be moved in to long term foster care, and given his behaviour right now I don't even dare think about what might happen after that.

But can I just accept that this is it? That regardless of what happens next, whether our therapy works or not, whether we get any additional help from social services or not, that this is what our life is going to be now? Can we accept the possibility that he is going to get worse, and be OK with that? What would happen if he was 16 and still violent on this scale?

Today I feel like I can't do this. Tomorrow I will probably pick myself up and have another go. I'm really not sure how many more times I can do that. Today, for the first time, I have allowed myself to imagine what it might feel like to live a life without Tickle in it.'

I CRIED FOR SIX HOURS that day. Really, properly cried. Sobbed, howled, rocked, wailed. I was devastated at the thought of losing Tickle, at the thought of what would happen to him if we disrupted, and the life-long effect that would have for him, but I was absolutely wrung out. Nothing left to give.

After a while, I managed to calm down enough to get myself back together and do some thinking. I realised I have been feeling this way for a while. Not all the time, certainly, but I had noticed I was avoiding thinking about certain things, connecting with people, and generally feeling a bit hollow. I knew I needed to do something, but if I'm honest, I was scared that if I looked too closely at myself I'd start crying and wouldn't be able to stop. I had told myself I had to get on with it; I have got kids to feed, things to organise, work to do, I can't afford to break down, I have to keep going, keep going. I found myself withdrawing from Husband, not wanting to go to the place where he looks after me and I am vulnerable because it's too much, so I would go to a hard place where I snapped at him a bit, and cuddle myself up in my own duvet because cuddling him was too difficult.

As with most things, these feelings would come and go, and occasionally some of it spilled out, and I felt a bit better for a while, and then I could feel it building up again, or I just felt nothing. The worst days were the ones where I had to mentally tell the muscles in my face to move in to a smile, or when Fairy cuddled me and I felt itchy all over and couldn't bear being touched.

On that day when I broke, I was crying because I knew that we weren't coping with Tickle. In the few months before that I think there had been two days where he hadn't hit one of us. We had just started seeing a new therapist, and pretty much the first thing she said to us, after we described what our life is like at home, is how *everything* and *everyone* is totally focused on Tickle and meeting his needs. She said that we do with him at home essentially what she would do in therapy – but 24 hours a day, seven days a week. With no training, no supervision, no respite. She was amazed and astonished at what we were doing.

Very tactfully, and gently, she suggested that perhaps we ought to be looking after ourselves a little bit as well.

Obviously, we knew about self-care. About taking time out to go for a walk, to watch *Holby City*, to do nice things for yourself. I have always been a bit of a workaholic – staying up with spreadsheets until 2.00am sort of thing, but I'd knocked all that on the head, so all good, right?

That day, I realised I really hadn't got self-care at all.

Self-care is not an add-on. It is not painting your nails once a month. It is *the key*. it is *everything*.

Before we adopted Tickle, and I had my 2.00am spreadsheets, I did used to get stressed, and get ill, and realise I was working too hard, and try and give myself a break. Burning the candle at both ends was my favourite hobby; I have always done it, always thrown myself in to things head on and immersed myself totally. Then every now and then I'd spend a week in my PJs with a box set of *Spooks*, and then off I'd go again.

This is a totally different league.

I approached adoption the same way I approach everything in life, and threw myself in to it wholeheartedly. I researched, I read books, I learned about therapeutic parenting, non-violent resistance, helping children voice their feelings, overcoming trauma. When Tickle arrived, I gave him everything I had.

With adoption, everything is focused around the child, and the child's needs. There are many obvious and good reasons for this. However, what was totally overlooked – in our case, and perhaps many others – was the needs of the adoptive parents.

Adoptive parenting is not like normal parenting. Sally Donovan calls it 'elite' parenting[3], and I'm inclined to agree. When you have a child who doesn't know what 'safe' feels like, who doesn't quite know if you're going to feed him today, who believes that adults hurt children, and that the momentary withdrawal of parental attention (e.g. to go to the toilet) looks the same as hours of neglect... handling that requires something over and above normal parenting.

Tickle needs me. He needs everything I have got, and more. He is going to need it for a really, really long time. Husband and I have given ourselves to him totally, and he has made huge progress since being with us; physically, emotionally, developmentally, educationally.

However, Tickle needs to re-learn *everything* he knows about the world. He spent five and a half years learning that the world was one way up, only to be told that was wrong. Black is actually white, up is down, *everything* he knows about *everything* is actually wrong.

It is going to take a lot of work for him to truly understand that the *real* world is the one where adults are kind, and look after you, and meet your needs. And how is he going to learn that?

From *me*. And from Husband.

So in that scenario, the most important people in that picture are, in fact, me and Husband, because if you take us away Tickle's tentative new world collapses and he has to start again from scratch, but this time with an added layer of trauma and rejection.

Currently, the only books I have read that place the adoptive parents at the heart of everything are Sally Donovan's books. I wish I'd found them sooner. The truth of the matter is, it doesn't matter how well we meet Tickle's needs, if Husband and I aren't cared for, if our needs aren't met, then this whole thing falls apart.

That Tuesday I thought I was crying because we can't meet Tickle's needs. I thought I would have to admit we can't cope. I thought that I couldn't keep Fairy safe with Tickle in the family. I thought we had failed him.

Looking back, I think I was crying because no one had met *my* needs. I had given all of myself to Tickle; I'd endured physical violence, I'd listened to him recount the abuse he'd suffered at the hands of someone who was supposed to care for him, I'd regulated his emotions for him almost constantly when he was unable to do it himself, I'd kept calm whilst being screamed at, I'd cuddled him after he'd hurt me and hurt my daughter, and told him thank you for saying sorry.

I was right that I couldn't cope, but what I had missed was *why* I couldn't.

I had given so much during the last 18 months, that on that day I had nothing left. On that day, I *couldn't* meet Tickle's needs, because I had nothing left to do it with.

Eventually, I came to realise that on the whole, Tickle's needs were being met very well indeed. But mine were not. And Husband's were not. And that was a problem.

Self-care, for me, since that day, has become the all and the everything.

I know for sure that if I don't get this right, then our family will fall apart. If I don't put myself first, every day, then I can't look after either of the children effectively. The Day I Broke opened my eyes to how worn down we had become. From that day, I forced myself to take my self-care to a whole new level. I know without a doubt that without it, we would crumble.

<u>The practicalities</u>

Self-care doesn't have to be complicated, expensive, or time consuming. In my house, the basics look like this:

- Eat three reasonably sensible meals every day. Utilise whatever resources you need in order to do this; whether it's supermarket deliveries, friends cooking for you, veg boxes, slow cookers, or a box of ingredients and instructions on what to do with them delivered to your house once a week. We have done all of the above and more, and at the moment survive on weekly HelloFresh deliveries.

- Get out and get moving. I have started walking back from school drop off the long way round; it adds about 20 minutes on to my school run but when I do it regularly I really notice the difference in how I feel. I also bought a Fitbit, and found it really interesting to track my movement and my sleep – and I did find it made me want to get up and move more.

· I do a yoga class twice a week. This won't be for everyone but for me it's amazing. One hour where my mind is totally focused on something other than my children (usually on how much pain my thighs are in) feels almost cleansing. Yoga is now a fixture in my weekly schedule, and I fit other things around it.

· Do a load of washing every couple of days. It's almost embarrassing to admit how full my basket gets, and when we keep reasonably on top of it (well, at least so it's not overflowing) I always feel a bit more in control of life.

· Play some music. Again, this is not for everyone, but I'm a musician and when I'm stressed I hardly ever play. At the time of writing this I had taken up the challenge of learning the tenor horn from scratch, so the novelty of a new instrument (and the fact that it's part of a sponsored charity event) made me much more likely to pick it up and practice. Maybe your therapy might be art, creative writing, dance, hiking – just find something that makes you feel like you again. For Husband, we make sure he gets a good long run in every weekend, and he does a few short ones in his lunch breaks during the week.

· Sleep. I'm not always brilliant at prioritising this, as I'm a night owl by nature and my brain is often whirring away just when I'm trying to nod off. But I know I should try.

- Counselling. I wish we had sorted this sooner, but Husband and I now see a counsellor once a week (in addition to Tickle's therapy) just to talk about us and how we're feeling. Sometimes it feels like the only time in the week where we have a proper conversation with each other. Even if you feel fine, I would urge you to do this; trauma can throw up issues for everyone, and it's much better to be prepared and have your support team in place.

The bottom line is, if you can build in self-care from the get-go, you are going to find this journey so much easier.

<u>The cup theory</u>

Once you have got yourself sorted and well cared for, then you can start to think about some small adjustments that will make a big difference to your everyday life – and which hopefully will help to reduce the amount of stress coming your way in the first place.

Imagine you have a cup, and the contents of the cup represent stress. Everyone will have a little bit in the bottom of their cup, just from normal life – work stress, friendship problems, money worries, or whatever. If some additional stress is added to the cup (maybe there was a lot of traffic on the way to work, you're feeling a bit unwell, or someone has used the last teabag, etc) it fills up a bit more, and a bit more, until eventually it may reach the top or even overflow. The important thing in this scenario is the gap between the level of your baseline 'stress' and the top of the cup – this is effectively your buffer zone, an idea of how much additional stress you could reasonably cope with and still be basically OK.

People who have experienced a traumatic event will have a significantly higher baseline stress level, possibly even a cup that is full or nearly full. Their buffer zone is totally erased, and this can mean that even the tiniest amount of stress can send them over the edge. Some days Tickle will go into complete meltdown just because he can't get his cars to go in a straight line.

I have found the idea of the stress cup really interesting, and really useful in terms of visualising and describing the realities of our everyday situation; in other words, how the tiniest upset can send our day completely out of kilter. Sometimes children are labelled attention-seeking or immature, because they cry at the 'slightest thing', or make a fuss over 'nothing'. The cup theory is key in helping us to understand what's going on for our children every single day, and in helping them to deal with it.

We all need a buffer zone to manage the normal day-to-day stresses of life (#ParentsHaveCupsToo). The fact that our children have a significantly reduced buffer will severely impact on their ability to cope with the normal ups and downs of daily life. The fact that we are managing a traumatised child on a daily basis will have an impact on *our* ability to cope with the normal ups and downs of daily life.

In a nutshell, this is what we mean when we talk about resilience. The ability to successfully cope with *stuff*. When you have suffered abuse, trauma, and neglect, your resilience is lowered. When you have a traumatised child living in your house, your resilience is lowered.

So, with the cup theory in mind, an obvious course of action is to try and reduce additional stresses – both on the child and on yourself, and at the same time, look at improving your coping skills, access to positive resources, and generally building resilience. Reducing stress on the child almost acts as a pre-emptive strike when it comes to our own self-care, and you can apply exactly the same theory to yourself and your stress points.

Reducing stress

We all know we're supposed to be therapeutic and nurturing, but faced with the same daily grind it can be hard. Child to Parent Violence (CPV) is a Real Thing in the adoption world, and in my house. As a parent, when you're under this sort of pressure every single day it can be *really* hard to keep up the super-therapeutic-nurturing-empathetic side of you. Your cup is filling up.

From my own experience, I have often found that the default place for me to go when my cup is full and Tickle is still hurting me is the one where I just feel angry with him; I want him to stop hurting me, I want him to go away and leave me alone. I blame him for hurting me. Sometimes it's obviously The Monster rather than Tickle, but at other times I have really been convinced Tickle is totally present and making that decision himself. As time goes on I'm less sure about this. I am starting to think The Monster is sneakier than I first thought.

Anyway, following the cup theory back logically: I want the CPV to stop, or at least reduce. The CPV happens when Tickle's cup overflows. Therefore, a way to get immediate results is to do what I can to stop his cup from overflowing.

It's a little bit of a switch around in thinking from 'traditional' behaviour modification parenting, and you might worry that from the outside, you appear to be rewarding bad behaviour; not only by not punishing or sanctioning the child, but by taking away other things that the child doesn't like and generally making their life easier. I suspect that some schools may instinctively take this line. However, when you look at things from the cup theory perspective, it makes perfect sense. Our children aren't acting this way out of spite, or because they're bad children. Their cup is overflowing and they can't cope.

Behaviour zones

The idea of choosing your battles is not a new one when it comes to parenting. It was recommended on the CAMHS course I attended to try to divide behaviours in to categories, or zones: non-negotiable, desirable, and don't-worry-about-it. (This is also a core component of the Non-Violent Resistance[4] model, if you've come across that.) This is vital for our own sanity; we as parents also have fairly full cups at the moment, so it's important to use our energy effectively, and focus on the important things, i.e. the non-negotiable behaviour. It's also a double whammy; as we become more relaxed about behaviours, our children become more relaxed too.

Examples of non-negotiable behaviours could be violence, shouting, spitting, attending school, personal hygiene... the list is endless, and it's personal to each family. Some things that might be in my non-negotiable zone could well be in your desirable category.

Desirable behaviours are the ones that you ideally would like to cultivate, but they aren't that important right now. Maybe they're something you'd like to have sorted within a year or so. Could be things like tidying up after themselves, piles of clothes on the floor, table manners, homework, etc. If you've got the energy on a given day, then go for it, but if not don't worry.

The don't-worry-about-it zone is the key to your mental health. Some stuff just isn't worth bothering about. Elbows off the table, tuck your shirt in, don't talk with your mouth full, put your toys away, help around the house.

Let it go. Conserve your energy to focus on the big stuff. It's helpful to you, but also means your child doesn't have 101 things they are being told off about throughout the day, and to an extent this should help stem the constant drip-drip-drip into their cup.

As part of this discussion during the CAMHS course we also talked a bit about older children; a couple of people had teenagers, and one lady in particular was worried that her daughter had more school work than she could cope with. The course leader was amazingly practical, and suggested focusing on a few subjects which are going to have an impact on her daughter's future. She (very bluntly!) said 'Is having GCSE history going to be any use to her in the future? No? Bin it.' Ruthless! Instead, she suggested focusing on the core subjects, plus one or two extra which the teenager would enjoy, to help give her a boost.

It's important to be aware that most schools would probably resist this; to them the most important thing is the number of A*–C grades that in that exam year, but to your child, it''s not going to make much difference in life if she's only got six GCSE's instead of eight or ten – as long as she's got the important ones. Plus, if she wants to, she can choose to go back to college later. The most important thing (in trauma healing terms) is what she is dealing with *right now* and how that is affecting her *right now* and what we can do about it *right now*.

Getting other people (schools, family members, friends) to understand your behaviour zones is crucial, and potentially quite tricky. However, consistency is going to be essential, as if the child knows that a certain behaviour is acceptable at home but they get told off for it when they go to Gran's, all that is going to do is add more stress to the cup.

It might seem odd or counterproductive that I started off this chapter saying I was talking about self-care, and for the last few pages I have ended up talking about the kids. However, if you are really building self-care in to your life, then this is a really important part of it. It's no good taking a weekend away from your family and then coming back and shouting at the children again, letting yourself get triggered by their behaviour, and building all that stress up again. Remember, we are not normal parents. We *have* to deal with things in a different way, and understanding how to create an environment at home which allows you to look after yourself at the same time as dealing with your child's needs is crucial to your ongoing wellbeing.

Don't get me wrong – I haven't found it easy to put myself first. Even knowing all of this, I still often get it wrong. Even when there are two of you, when you're both feeling the grind and you both want the other one to take over for a minute it can be tough, or when your mum has helped so much that she is fed up with the lot of you and your only back-up plan fades away.

When Husband and I find ourselves arguing about who is the most tired and most deserving of the lie in, what usually works best for us is to pair up and do it together. Tag-teaming is our normal game, and works well when one of us feels awake enough to take Tickle out of the house and do something with him, but when we're both exhausted it makes it worse; the one who takes Tickle out usually keels over way before the one who's supposed to be recovering has had a chance to do more than go to the loo in peace. On those days, we prop each other up. Take the kids to soft play and silently hold hands as we whimper over a cup of cheap lemonade. On the days when it's just me and Husband was at work, I'd do my best to get out of the house and meet up with a friend. Somehow just having someone else there with me really helped.

I said I was going to be blunt and brutal, so here it is: you will not survive this journey without looking after yourself. If you take nothing else from this book, please believe me on that. It is simply not possible. You are important, and you are worth it. For your child, and for you.

From the blog

Fear

My life is ruled by fear at the moment. It's pervasive; it affects everything.

I got bitten this morning, because of it. Because Tickle was throwing stuff around, and I grabbed his arm from behind and surprised him, and he thought I was going to hurt him. He bit me on instinct, pure self-preservation.

Afterwards he was completely freaked out. If I'd thought about it, I would have expected him to go loopy, or need restraining, but he didn't. He was really shocked at himself. He kept trying to explain what had happened, but not quite having the right words; asking to look at the bite mark on my arm, rubbing and kissing it better. He said sorry without being asked. He was on the verge of tears.

Last night Tickle was able to articulate what we have known for a long time. He's scared of going to sleep because he thinks someone will come in and hurt him. He is terrified that his birth parent will come to our house; it doesn't matter how many times I tell him that they don't know where we live, he makes me promise over and over that I will send them away and not let them in the house.

Sometimes it's difficult to keep putting one foot in front of the other. I keep going, and mostly manage to think about other things, but it just builds up inside. It's weighing heavy on my heart today.

3 The Brain

When Tickle was first presented to us as a potential match, he was described as a child who would probably grow up to have a moderate learning disability. If I'm honest, didn't really know what that meant. I understood the words, obviously, but 'learning disability' is quite a broad term, and despite having worked with children with special needs on and off for a few years, I couldn't visualise in my head what having a child with a 'moderate learning disability' would feel like, or how it would affect our family. I dealt with this, on the most part, by not really thinking about it. It was probably quite a naïve way of doing it, but I just focused on Tickle, day by day. On dealing with what he was like in the moment, how he was behaving, interacting, communicating on that day. And bit by bit, naïve as it may have been, it led me to believe that Tickle didn't have the level of disability that we'd been told, but that he was a little boy who had suffered extreme trauma.

It took quite a long time to figure all this out, and even longer to convince his social worker of it. I have said to more than one social worker that Tickle is anxious, frightened, worried, only to have the response come back 'What's he got to be frightened of?'. This idea that once the child is placed in a loving family all their problems disappear is generally accepted as an extremely outdated view of adoption, but unfortunately it's one that still prevails, even it seems, amongst some professionals. I think it's fair to say that in our case, and in lots of others I know about, there was a huge gap in the social workers' understanding of trauma and how it affects children who are placed for adoption.

To understand this better, it helps to go back to basics, and take a look at how our brains work.

Your brain is an amazing thing. I only know a small amount about a very small part of it, and even just that tiny bit is fantastically complex and wonderful. However, as well as being hugely sophisticated, it can also be surprisingly simplistic at times; in fact, some regions of our brain have stayed almost exactly the same over millions of years of evolution.[5] At a very basic level, your brain considers itself to have one job – to keep you alive. It doesn't matter to your brain that humans are top of the food chain and it's unlikely that a bear will suddenly leap out from behind a tree, all of these instinctive danger response mechanisms that would have been vital to keep our ancestors alive are still doing exactly the same job as they always have, even though we don't really need them to. This means that in certain conditions, the higher-functioning parts of our brain can be completely hijacked by the older, lower regions, as the brain prioritises our survival. When we're thinking about our adopted children, and their disproportionate responses to everyday occurrences, I've found it really helpful to have a bit of an understanding of how our brain works in these situations.

The Triune Brain

I'm a big fan of Jane Evans, who has done some great work on the brain which is really accessible for children as well as adults[6]. In her talks, Jane explains that there three key areas of the brain which are relevant to trauma processing; she uses an analogy of a meerkat, an elephant, and a monkey. The meerkat is your first responder, always on the look-out for danger; the elephant is responsible for processing and storing memories, and the monkey is the logical, rational one who does all the thinking.

Jane's ideas stem from a theory called the 'Triune Brain', meaning 'three in one'. It was first developed in the 1960s by an American neuroscientist called Paul MacLean[7]. In reality, it's a bit more complex than the theory accounts for, but it still provides a sound basis for starting to think about how the brain affects behaviour. Below I've tried to simplify some of the key areas of the brain and explain how they are linked to trauma behaviours.

1) The brain stem. Also sometimes called the reptilian brain[8], or the hind brain. This is the oldest bit of the brain, and deals with the most basic and instinctive responses and threats to survival, as well as bodily functions such as breathing and digestion. It's this part of the brain that controls the nervous system, so will instantly calculate that the surface I have just placed my hand on is red hot and instruct my arm to remove my hand from the surface before I have even consciously noticed what I'm doing.

2) The limbic system, also known as mammalian brain. There are a number of areas within the limbic system, but two that are particularly important to the understanding of trauma are the amygdala and the hippocampus. The amygdala is the part that Jane Evans refers to as the meerkat. It's an alarm system, on the lookout for danger, and its job is to alert you to anything it thinks might be a threat. It processes things quickly and instinctively, and it acts to keep you safe at all times. In the terms we like to think about it in our house, it is the amygdala which powers The Monster. The hippocampus is what Jane calls the elephant brain, and it's key for storing memories. The mammalian brain is sometimes referred to as the 'emotional' brain; it contains structures which are important in social activities; how I manage relationships, do I fit in with my peers, am I part of the tribe? I recently came across the concept of a 'social threat' – mammals are social animals, and there is usually safety in numbers. A social threat may be that I am away from the rest of my pack, and therefore am more vulnerable; it may not be an immediate threat to life, but it's enough to make you uncomfortable and want to change your situation.

3) The frontal lobes. This is the area known as the 'human' brain, or higher brain.[9] It's the higher brain that Jane Evans refers to when she uses the metaphor of the monkey brain. This is the intelligent, planning, thinking, logical part of the brain. My friend Chris likes to refer to it as the human brain because it's where all the planning, goal setting, and thinking happens, and we're the only species that actually does any of that. Can you imagine a gorilla setting a goal to have eaten twenty bananas by next Tuesday?!

In survival terms, there's a hierarchy to these bits of the brain: because the amygdala (meerkat) is the part that deals with immediate threats to life, it instantly takes over if it senses any threat, and the higher brain functions are put on standby mode. It's efficient and instinctive, and means that all of your body's resources can be instantly deployed where they are most needed, in order to keep you alive. The amygdala can trigger our fight/flight/freeze/appease responses, allowing us to respond instinctively to threat without having to take the time to think it through consciously. In later chapters we will explore some strategies for managing children when their meerkat brain is engaged.

The developing brain

As I mentioned earlier, the way the brain develops is a large and complex subject, and if I'm really honest, I don't know the half of it. However, I'm going to pick on one small (simplified) aspect, to help illustrate some of the difficulties our children will have.

At a very basic level, babies are genetically designed to get their needs met. They are cute and cuddly, so attract adults to them, just to coo over them. They are charming and engaging, and they cry or scream to let you know they are unhappy. In the baby's developing brain there is a cycle which goes something like this:

AS THE BABY HAS HIS or her needs met consistently by their caregiver/s, there are connections building in the brain about safety, trust, how the world works, the role of adults, the role of the baby, how to regulate emotions and so on. However, if the baby *doesn't* regularly have their needs met, the brain will build connections of a very different type: I'm not safe, I am not being looked after, there's no point crying, nobody is meeting my needs. It's worth noting that this process of learning and brain growth doesn't stop with babies, but 90 percent of the brain's growth will happen in the first five years of life[10], so those early months and years are incredibly important in shaping the way that the brain grows.

Tickle, like many other 'looked-after' children, has a brain which is programmed to look out for danger. His early experiences taught him that adults are not safe; they can hurt you, they withhold food and drink, they don't respond to your needs, they do things that make you scared. Growing up in that environment has physically shaped the way Tickle's brain has developed.

The brain and childhood trauma

Dr Ruth Lanius in the USA did a really interesting experiment in her lab[11]. She showed her participants a picture of a person with a lovely smiling face, and at the same time scanned their brains to see which bits were active. When she did this with people who hadn't suffered trauma, the scans showed lots of activity in the pre-frontal cortex (the human brain). However, when she showed the same picture to people who had suffered from trauma, the activity was all in the brain stem. The amygdala (or the little meerkat if you like that analogy) had detected a possible threat, the activity in the human brain had ceased, and the older, instinctive parts of the brain had taken charge. Why did that happen? Because the brain has been programmed to look out for threats, and has detected something in that picture that has previously meant danger. It could be an abuser who always smiled before they started. It could be that showing happiness was punished. I heard once of a trauma patient who was triggered every time the therapist raised her eyebrows. There is no logical process to this, and it's not something the person is consciously doing, or even aware of. It's a survival instinct as finely honed as the meerkat who senses that first whiff of danger in their surroundings.

Memory and the nervous system

The nervous system in our body controls all of our instinctive responses, and all of our senses. It's the system that is responsible for carrying messages from the brain all over the body, so it seems logical that when you have a brain that is shaped by trauma, the whole body can end up carrying it. I see this very vividly in Tickle's body – his muscles are permanently rock solid, and there is not an ounce of squidge on him anywhere.

Memory is a big and complex topic in psychology, but for the purpose of this section I'm going to home in on one particular type. 'Procedural memory' is a form of long-term memory that is responsible for 'knowing how to do things'. For example, when you learn to drive a car, or ride a bike, or even walk, at first you have to really think about what you're doing, but as you get better at it, it becomes automatic. This is procedural memory: your body remembering how to do these things without you consciously telling it how and when to move. You could think about it as a 'habit' that your nervous system has got in to.

Procedural memory is important when considering trauma that is 'stuck' in our bodies and in our nervous systems, as it applies to behaviours learned from trauma and traumatic situations in the same way as the ones learned in other 'normal' situations – or indeed skills that we are deliberately attempting to learn. For example, if someone has developed a habit of always shrinking away from confrontation to try to make themselves small, the body learns to exist like this without even thinking about it. If you have a physical trauma in the body, such as a broken limb, the rest of your body will adapt, and sometimes even after the limb is healed you might find you have to 're-train' your body to move as it did before.

When someone is exposed to a traumatic situation, there is a great deal of 'energy' in the body as the fight or flight response is triggered. If the person is prevented from fighting, or fleeing – either they are physically unable to escape or they perceive that they are unable to escape – then the person is not able to complete the fight or flight action, which would release the energy from the body.[12] The energy generated by the uncompleted fight or flight action then becomes 'stuck' in the body.

This understanding of procedural memory provides us with a theory as to why Tickle's muscles are always tense; years of Tickle's nervous system being triggered by perceived (or actual) dangers in his environment have built up until Tickle's tight muscles become a physical manifestation of the trauma he carries in his body. Even though he may not be able to verbalise what has caused the trauma, it lives on in his body as procedural memory.

Traumatic memories

On to a slightly different type of memory. Whereas procedural memories are ones that we are rarely conscious of, we also have conscious recollections of past experiences, which are known as 'episodic' memories (i.e. memory of an 'episode', a thing that happened). Obviously we can have 'good' memories and 'bad' memories, all of which are stored and processed within the brain. However, traumatic memories are stored and processed *completely differently* from other memories, even from other unpleasant ones. They are often fragmented, have gaps, and are poorly contextualised – in other words they don't seem to apply to any particular situation, they could have happened anywhere, at any time[13]. Because they are not 'time tagged', when a person remembers that event, it will feel to them like it is happening in the here and now.

In a nutshell: Traumatic memories are stored differently in the brain, so that when you experience a traumatic memory it feels as if it was happening right now.

Traumatic memories are recognised as threatening by the amygdala, so not only is the memory being experienced as if it's happening right now, your reptilian brain has gone in to red alert and is preparing your body to deal with the threat (in our case, firing up The Monster). Thinking back to the hierarchy in the brain, when the amygdala is triggered, the higher brain functions shut down, leaving the person unable to think or feel things consciously. Tickle's Monster has total control, and Operation Save Tickle From Impending Danger has been launched.

What can sometimes be difficult to comprehend is that this doesn't just happen when a person *chooses* to think about the trauma that's occurred. Triggers in a person's environment can provoke flashbacks, and often they will find it impossible to say what has caused the memory to resurface. The first time Tickle saw his therapist he kept saying he was frightened by the way she leant forwards over her knees. This morning he said to me he didn't like the way my head was leaning over to one side.

Dissociation

I spoke a bit about what dissociation looks like for us in chapter 1. It took a really long time for us to understand what was happening, but we've since found out it's quite common for people who have suffered trauma to dissociate, or simply 'tune out' of their environment.

Psychologists describe dissociation as the brain 'shutting down'. For me, it always seemed like whatever was going on in Tickle's head was too painful, so he climbed inside a little box in the corner of his head and let The Monster take over until it was safe again.

Dissociating is, in itself, traumatic. Tickle often has very few memories of what he has done whilst in a dissociative state, and is mostly confused by what he does remember. When you can't integrate your memories and make sense of them it can affect your sense of who you are, where you came from, and trying to understand the story of your own life can be utterly bemusing. You can't rely on your own memories or experiences. This can impact on the self concept – by which I mean how a child thinks about themselves, as an individual person, separate from other people. Can they tell you anything about themselves? What they like doing? What colour eyes they have? Can they tell you about their family, and how they fit in to that? Their sister/brother?

I worked with a boy once in a mainstream primary school, with no identified learning needs, but who was displaying challenging behaviour. I remember asking him, tell me something about you? No response. What do you like doing? Don't know. In the end, I had to ask him individually, do you like football? Do you like cooking? Do you like reading? And only then was he able to answer me. Following this idea through, how can you ever expect a child to develop positive self-esteem if they have no concept of themselves in the first place?

In order for our children to cope with the traumatic memories, we need to find a way of bringing other brain areas back in to play, so they are not left at the mercy of their amygdala. The traumatic event needs to be put in context, separated from current reality, and properly stored as a memory of something that *has* happened, not *is* happening. This is a long-term strategy, but it's worth it.

In summary, at the moment Tickle is experiencing traumatic memories, which can be triggered by anything in his environment, or appear in his mind unbidden. He's not remembering them like you or I would remember what we had for dinner last night, he is experiencing them as if they were happening to him right now. He's feeling the same emotions, and the same feelings in his body as he felt when the event happened, and his body remembers the trauma, even when he's not consciously thinking about it. In order to move on, Tickle needs to be able to form a story, or narrative of the memory so that he can think about it from a detached, third-party point of view. He needs to retrain his body to move in different ways. He needs to take charge of The Monster, and learn to sit with his uncomfortable feelings instead of escaping from them.

It's quite a lot to ask, isn't it?

It does seem pretty stark, laid out like that, and I don't want to dishearten you. It *is* a big task to take on, but forewarned is definitely forearmed, and the more you can learn about the reasons behind your child's behaviour the easier it will be for you to manage your own responses to it, and to find new ways of helping them.

Starting to address the issues that come hand in hand with trauma can feel like a daunting task, but can be broken down in to two distinct approaches – firstly dealing with the immediate 'challenging behaviour', and secondly embedding some longer-term strategies to slowly shift the habits, physiology, and feelings of your child.

From the blog

Dissociation

This morning Tickle was worried about school, as usual.

At breakfast he was banging the table, and saying he wanted to hurt the cats. Each time I asked him to come in to the sitting room with me, to have a sit in the comfy chair and calm down. The first time I said I had to keep Etta safe, as he's not allowed to hurt her; he has to come and sit with me until he has calmed down and I know he's not going to hurt her. The second time, I said he wasn't allowed to bang on the table but he could bang on the comfy chair if he wanted, which he did, until he said 'I have had enough of banging' and went to finish his breakfast.

So far so good.

*Then came the time when he would usually watch a bit of TV and wait for the taxi, but he'd already thrown the TV remote across the room earlier on (I am abbreviating our morning quite a lot; he'd also woken at 1.00am, 4.00am, and 5.00am, and Husband was in a bit of a state) so I had told him that it was 'broken' and he wouldn't be able to watch any Bing today (*what *a shame). He was a bit annoyed, but we'd already had the discussion earlier (along with the shouting) so at the time he pretty much just got on with playing with his cars on the floor. Fairy and I were sitting at the table at this point, and she was having her breakfast. Then, suddenly, he just popped up behind her, whacked her on the head and pulled at her hair.*

Husband was still here at this point so he went to Fairy and I grabbed Tickle. This is the sort of situation where previously I would have gone straight in to a time in, and held him on the sofa. Perhaps that would have been the better thing to do today, perhaps he needed me close to calm down.

However, what I actually did was suggest that Tickle go up to his room for some calm down time, and Fairy (who wouldn't leave my side) and I would go upstairs and have a picnic on the landing to finish our breakfast. There was a lot of screaming. Each time he screamed I closed his bedroom door, explaining that I didn't like the noise, and he could open it when he'd finished screaming. [Tickle opens door, screams, repeats...] We kept this up for a while, Fairy was wearing a spare pair of ear defenders, Tickle pulled my hair, etc. He eventually calmed enough to stop screaming, and I asked if he would like me to come in and help him to calm down. He said yes, I came in to his room, he screamed some more.

Eventually, after we had agreed that I would leave the room if he continued to scream, he calmed enough to ask for a squeeze, and we had a few. He seemed a bit calmer. Then he ramped up again. By this point I was feeling a bit narked, to say the least, so I explained to him that I was feeling cross so I was going to my room to calm down a bit. (Husband and I had decided we would try to model this for him!) Needless to say, that set him off even more, and he managed to grab Fairy again on her way into my room.

Fairy and I sat on the floor in my bedroom. I felt safe. I felt Fairy was safe. It was a bigger relief than I had expected.

Everything went quiet outside, and then there was a little voice at the door. 'Mummy! The taxi is here.' 'OK,' I said, 'let's go and put your shoes on.'

'I DON'T WANT TO GO TO SCHOOL!'

I don't quite remember how we got downstairs, but we did, and I got his shoes on. The escort was standing at the door, chatting to him, talking about how he would be OK at school. Then I went to get his school bag, and all hell broke loose. He ran in to the sitting room, where there was a massive pile of clean washing on the sofa. He pushed it all off on to the floor. And all the blankets. Then he climbed on to the sofa and jumped on it like a trampoline, screeching like a banshee.

I went to the kitchen to get him a snack for his school bag. At this point, Fairy appeared downstairs, wanting to bring her breakfast bowl to put in the kitchen. Tickle went for her. As I heard her scream I turned around to see her bent double, with Tickle hanging off her hair with both hands.

I grabbed him. I put my other arm around her. I shouted at him. I wasn't out of control, but I needed him to see I was angry. He was quite interested in me shouting. He told me he didn't like it, calm as anything. That sounds like a positive, but it's not – Fairy was sobbing in to my shoulder, I was yelling at him, and he was stood there, calm as you like, going 'Oh look, Mummy's shouting.'

The poor escort is still waiting at the door, having to listen to all this. I let go of Fairy, and take Tickle over to her. I explain to Tickle that he has not got a snack today, because as I was trying to find one he had hurt Fairy, and so I wasn't able to get him one. I have no idea what they will make of that at school, but there you go.

I shoved him at the escort, told him I'd see him later, and said have a nice day. 'Bye Mummy!' he called. 'Have a nice day too!'

I mean, what can you do with that? It's like he is not inhabiting the same reality as we are. Which I know is probably true, in some ways, but it's incredibly hard to know what to do about it when you are right in the thick of it.

4 Dealing with 'challenging behaviours'

The first time Tickle bit me was about six weeks after he'd been placed with us. At the time it was a huge shock. It hurt so much. Husband immediately went into overprotective mode, ordered me out of the room, and did the whole of bedtime himself while I sat in our bedroom and cried. In the aftermath of the bite, I took refuge in my usual coping strategy, and went in to research mode. There's a lot of parenting advice on the internet (as any confused new parent can tell you) and I spent the evening poring over any article that looked like it would give me a clue on how to deal with a child who bites.

When Tickle came to us we were told by his social worker that he was displaying 'challenging behaviours' and he needed clear boundaries. Her reasoning for this was that he didn't have clear or consistent boundaries at home, and that these boundaries would make him feel more secure, and therefore less likely to misbehave. All of which sounds perfectly sensible, but is perhaps something of a simplistic viewpoint.

Guided by the social workers, our main strategies in the early days were based on behaviour modification. You might have come across the 'naughty step' model of parenting (although we never used that particular gem). In this approach, if there is a behaviour you want to change, the child is sanctioned when they display the unwanted behaviour, and rewarded when they behave in the way you want them to. For a child with a trauma background, however, this is unlikely to be hugely successful.

It's not true to say that these strategies didn't work at all, because they did: when Tickle was calm, settled, and able to think through the choices he wanted to make. He's an intelligent child, and he's quite capable of figuring out the link between good behaviour and nice treats. However, the times when it didn't work were the times when he wasn't able to think clearly, when his brain had flipped the switch in to loopy mode, and all he was capable of doing was running around screaming and trying to find an outlet for all his pent-up emotional panic.

The Monster does not respond well to behaviour management strategies. Behaviour management strategies have nothing to do with Tickle's safety, and that is all The Monster is concerned about. Think back to the fight/flight/freeze scenario that is triggered by the amygdala – reactions are instinctive and unconscious, because your brain is responding to a perceived danger, and if you take the time to stop and think it through that could be the difference between surviving and not. Taking away a toy is not going to have any effect on Tickle in this state of arousal, because his brain is locked in to survival mode.

It's difficult to phrase this next bit without sounding like a preachy self-discovery book, but it was at this point in my post-bite musings that I guiltily realised we'd been doing the one thing that I most hate – we had been focusing entirely on Tickle's behaviour and ignoring all the feelings and needs that were underpinning it.

Fairy is a bit 'naughty' sometimes, but she is perfectly able to accept the consequences (even if she doesn't like them) and regulate her own emotional state. If she's upset, she likes to take herself off to her bedroom to calm down, and she *knows* that when she's ready Husband and I will be there with hugs and kisses. Our love for her is not in question in her mind, she knows it is a constant. But what if that wasn't such a certainty? What if misbehaviour was associated with violence, withdrawal of love, or food? Suddenly, the child is at risk of danger, the meerkat brain goes on alert, and the body is flooded with adrenaline, ready for fight or flight.

Time in

In the course of my post-bite research I found a few articles on 'gentle' parenting which got me thinking, and I decided to try something different. If Tickle started misbehaving, instead of moving 'away' from him, I would move 'towards' him. This isn't the same as rewarding bad behaviour, but addressing the behaviour in a way that keeps Tickle feeling safe and helps to calm and regulate him. When Tickle hit, shouted, or did anything that would have warranted a sanction, then instead he would get a two minute 'time out' sat on my lap. There is still a consequence for his behaviour, as he's not allowed to play during that time, but instead of feeling rejected he is in a place where he is safe and loved. In the adoption world, this is usually known as a 'time in'.

When I first attempted this approach, Tickle would often kick and scream like mad, and I would have to hold him in a tight hug, or hold on to his hands to stop him from hitting me. If you're going to do this, it's important to explain to the child what you are doing, or they could perceive you as trying to hurt or control them. I usually say things like 'Mummy is just giving you a big cuddle to help you calm down' or 'Mummy needs to hold your hands for a moment Tickle, so that you can't hit anyone. I need to keep everyone safe. When you are calm and don't need to hit any more then I can let go.'

About a week in to using this new approach Tickle was responding really well, and was able to calm down fairly quickly, say sorry, and play nicely after his two minutes was up.

Over the years this has been a pretty steadfast method for helping Tickle to regulate his behaviours and feelings, and it's done us well, although he has tested it many times! One particular time Tickle was sat on my lap screaming; I was explaining to him that if he screamed he would have to sit for longer, until he had calmed down and sat nicely for two minutes. He screamed again, and then waited. I repeated what I'd just said. He screamed. I repeated. This went on for some time, with his screams gradually becoming quieter, until he eventually realised that there was no acceptable level of screaming, and no shortcut that would get him out of the time in any quicker!

I have found I need to tread carefully with this method however – it's important that it's not used as restraint but is about keeping Tickle (and the rest of the family) safe and helping him regulate his emotions. I don't use it as 'punishment' in the conventional sense, and I try to avoid saying things like 'If you bang the table again you'll get a time in'. For traumatised children it's important that they see a clear link between actions and consequences, and in the example above there is no logical reason given for why banging should lead to a time in. However, if I were to say 'You have just banged the table, which makes me think you might need some help calming down. I'd like you to come and sit with me on the sofa please, and I will help you to calm down' this gives a logical reason, and explanation for the sanction. Of course, he still resists it! In that scenario I would then follow up with something like 'Well my job is to keep you safe Tickle, and when you are banging it's not safe, as you could break the table or hurt your hand.'

As time has gone on, Tickle has learned that sitting with me or Husband does actually help him to calm down, and these days he will even ask for a cuddle or a chat if he's starting to get anxious. It won't work like that for all children, and for some it may take much longer than others, but whichever method you choose to use it's important to be clear and consistent. Explain what you are doing, and why, and apply it in the same way to every situation.

Our time ins with Tickle can vary quite a lot. Sometimes we just sit side by side, and I put my arm around him. At other times, to be perfectly honest, it feels like restraining. Sometimes I feel like I'm doing no better than the person who abused him in the first place. That's not an easy thing to write, and I have nearly deleted it four times, but I feel I need to be honest about this: it's not always pretty.

Social workers talk calmly about time ins like they are the obvious choice for loving, attentive, therapeutic parents, but I would be willing to bet that they have never done one with a child who is screaming and scratching at their face. Unfortunately there is no easy answer to this; my best advice is to make sure that you're staying present and aware of what you're doing, and if you feel like you're in danger of losing control then walk away. I try to stay calm, and only hold what I have to, for example if Tickle is punching me, then I have to hold his hands. If he is headbutting me the I will cradle his head until I feel the tension leave him. If in that moment I don't feel like I can do this safely, I know I need to get Tickle to a place where he won't hurt himself or anyone else, and then remove myself from the situation until I'm calm enough to deal with it.

Don't be afraid to change your approach

Our family went through a rough patch a few months ago, where Tickle's behaviour was escalating and we felt like things were getting out of hand. Our time ins had started to feel like restraint; neither Husband or I were comfortable with the situation, but we didn't know what else to do. Thankfully, we had been referred to therapy by this point, and our therapist was instrumental in helping us to realise that we'd come to rely on time in as our go-to method, and it had become more of a power struggle than a regulating technique. For Husband and I, trying to stay calm while holding Tickle (who would be attempting to bite or headbutt us) was detrimental to our mental health, and Tickle would fight against us as we tried to keep him under control. The only reason we were able to maintain the upper hand was because we were physically stronger than him.

When I thought about it, the time ins had been such a game-changer when we first introduced them that we had become too reliant on them. As Tickle changed and developed, the way we were doing them became less effective, but because we knew they had worked in the past, we kept going and just tried harder. Initially, one of the main reasons for time ins was to help build a bond between ourselves and Tickle, and not leave Tickle feeling like he'd been abandoned. However, as his attachment grew he didn't need this in quite the same way, and the time in started to feel constraining for him. The harder he resisted, the harder we tried to keep him there, because we simply didn't know what else to do, and had no spare brainpower to think of a new strategy.

There was one important thing our therapist said to break this cycle: sometimes it's OK to do something because it's the right thing for Husband and me, even if it's not necessarily the right thing for Tickle.

In our efforts to be the best parents we could be, we had allowed Tickle and his needs to dominate our lives 24 hours a day. Although perhaps commendable, it is simply not sustainable. Our therapist gave us permission to step away and take a breath.

Space to calm

Being encouraged to think about our situation in terms of what was good for Husband and myself as well as what was good for Tickle allowed us to come up with some different ideas. There are lots of parents who are staunch advocates of the 'stay close' method, but having done some (extremely unscientific) research on Twitter, I found most of the people advocating that method had not encountered anything like the level of violence that we were experiencing at home. The people who could relate to what we were going through unfailingly spoke with one voice: Keep Yourself Safe.

It was at this point that we started to introduce the 'calming space' approach. If Tickle had a meltdown, then we would invite him to go up to his bedroom and have some time to calm down. Husband or I would accompany him, and either sit in his room with him, or, if it became unsafe for us (or if we'd just had enough) we would wait outside.

Husband and I each had to find the right way for us when dealing with this new situation. For me, the general rule was that I would go and stand just outside Tickle's room if he started screaming, and if he started throwing things at me I would close the door. I have moved 'breaking things' in to my don't-worry-about-it zone – as long as it is Tickle's things he's breaking! The day I described in chapter 1, where Tickle spent four hours tearing his room to pieces, was the first time I had felt confident enough to let it go that far. It was scary at times, not really knowing how much Tickle might push things before he stopped, and certainly to me he seemed to go right to the edge – but amazingly, he came back again. On that morning I stayed with Tickle throughout the whole episode; sitting outside his bedroom door, shutting it every time he opened it, and calmly repeating that I was going to keep the door shut while he was throwing things.

I honestly don't think this approach would have worked so well in the early days. When he first came to us Tickle would escalate at an alarming rate when left on his own, however, having built a basic level of trust and attachment with him, we began to find that we could sometimes leave him to calm down by himself.

All behaviour is communication

I don't know who it was who first said that all behaviour is communication, but if you can make that shift in your mindset to genuinely believe that statement then it can be a game-changer. Adopting this way of thinking enabled me to go from 'Why is Tickle hurting me?' to 'What does Tickle need to tell me that he's not able to say?' This in turn allowed me to respond in a totally different way to him when his behaviours were difficult.

One thing I frequently have to remind myself of is that in this moment, there is nothing *I* can do to control Tickle's behaviour. All I can control is my reaction to it. I don't have to feel like a failure because I can't 'make' him behave, 'make' him tidy up, 'make' him stop hitting, because short of physically restraining him it's not within my power to control another human being. What I *can* do, is control my own reactions to his behaviour, and model for Tickle how to manage and control his own behaviour in a more acceptable and safe way.

It may sound obvious, but we as parents are *the* role model for our children. If I shout at Tickle, I'm teaching him that shouting at each other is how we deal with situations when we feel angry. That's obviously not something I wanted to encourage, so I deliberately spent at least the first year that Tickle lived with us trying to squash my emotions whenever he was around. I would always try to speak in a calm voice, no matter how angry or frustrated I was. If he upset me, I would go in to another room and cry in secret. It wasn't until that first conversation with our therapist that I realised that in doing this, I was actually depriving Tickle of the opportunity to observe alternative strategies for dealing with negative emotions. His birth family had 'taught' him that when you are angry you shout, scream, and hit. I suddenly realised that the best way to reverse this lesson was to let Tickle see me doing something different. I started saying things like 'Mummy is feeling really cross at the moment, so I'm just going in to the other room to calm down' and 'Tickle, I do not like it when you shout at me. It makes me feel angry.'

Once, in a moment of frustration I said to him 'Mummy is really cross at the moment Tickle, but I'm still not going to hit you. I am cross with you, but I'm not going to hit you.'

He froze, and went completely silent. 'Are you?' he said. That was my lightbulb moment. Tickle was terrified that Husband and I were going to hurt him, and all the crazy behaviour, violence, and dissociation stemmed from that one fear. Eventually Tickle started to verbalise it for himself, and even to this day he will occasionally meet someone new and ask them 'Do you hurt?'

In the interest of full disclosure, I would like to point out here that sometimes I do lose my rag completely and yell at Tickle. I have come to realise that actually, that's OK too, because afterwards I say sorry, and Tickle can see that even when I do get *really* angry I still won't hit him. Feel what you feel. Repair if necessary. In my view, this is essentially what we're trying to teach our children to do, and it won't do them any harm to see that their parents are human – and fallible – too.

PACE

I'm going to go in to more detail in chapter 8 about supporting children to express their emotions, but for now I want to explore a few more ideas that may help when you're having a particularly difficult day. If you've not yet heard of PACE, then don't worry, you soon will have! It was developed by Dan Hughes[14], who is considered by many adopters as something akin to Jesus.

PACE describes a way of communicating with traumatised children; it stands for Playfulness, Acceptance, Curiosity, and Empathy. (I believe since it was first developed it has been updated to PLACE, with the L standing for Love.) Dan suggests that responding in this way to a child can significantly improve the quality of communication that you have with them, and I know a great many adopters and foster carers who would agree.

Curiosity: I wonder...?

Curiosity was the first stage for us. When Tickle came to live with us he only knew the emotions 'happy' and 'sad' and I'm not even sure he really understood those. One of the things we tried to do right from the start is to name his feelings for him.

'Tickle, it looks to me like you might be feeling sad. Do you think I'm right, or wrong?'

'Tickle, I wonder if you are feeling angry'

'You've just hit Mummy in the face Tickle, and that makes me think that you might be a bit cross.'

'You look like a happy Tickle!'

It's hard sometimes (see point 3, above) and it can be exhausting. But over time it has given Tickle a much larger vocabulary to talk about his feelings. He now tells me almost daily that he has 'dikka-fult' feelings, and whereas I initially had to 'wonder' about each individual feeling, he will now jump straight in to tell me that he has sad-sad-frightened-worried-and-sad.

You can use 'I wonder' for any situation where you suspect something, but don't want to put words in to your child's mouth. It's a really powerful tool – in the early days I frequently coupled it with 'Do you think I'm right or wrong?' so that Tickle was forced to make a choice, rather than simply saying 'yes' to whatever I said. As Tickle started to gain confidence with exploring his feelings I would 'wonder' whether they were feelings about something that had happened at our house, or might be feelings about something that had happened in a different house. Asking Tickle outright what he was feeling sad about would only elicit 'I don't know', but 'wondering' let me gently guide him through to find the source.

Acceptance and Empathy

Whatever Tickle throws at me in terms of emotions, I accept. I sympathise. I empathise.

'I can understand why you feel that way.'

'Poor Tickle, that must be really difficult.'

'If I were you, I think I'd feel sad too.'

'It's OK to feel angry.'

'Everyone feels scared sometimes.'

Acceptance is *so* important. Acceptance lets Tickle know that I hear him, that he is valued, and that his experiences and feelings are valid. I do not ever dismiss something that he has told me, even if it seems like nothing to me, or if I think he's making it up. Even if I *know* he's misinterpreted or got the wrong end of the stick, I still make a point to accept his version of events, before 'wondering' whether there might be an alternative explanation.

'Poor Tickle, it must have made you feel very sad when Dad was cross with you. I wonder why Dad was cross? Do you think it might be because you had just headbutted him? Perhaps if you hadn't headbutted Dad then he might not have been cross? It is sad though, isn't it, and sometimes it's very hard not to headbutt people.'

Acceptance is even more vital when it comes to disclosures. The very first thing I ever do when Tickle tells me something that has happened to him is show him I believe him. Tell him that it wasn't his fault, and it shouldn't have happened. That I would feel angry and sad if it happened to me. It's amazing the confidence this has given him; I often hear my own words reflected back at me as he chats things through to process them.

In our family, what has developed naturally out of this naming of feelings is an array of alternative strategies for dealing with them. For example, we often say to Tickle that it's OK to be angry, but it's not OK to hit. If you're angry, I wonder what you could do instead to help get those feelings out? Could you hit a pillow? Could you throw some cuddly toys on to your bed? Could you squeeze a rubber ball very hard? Could you stamp your feet?

Playfulness

Playfulness can be a lovely thing to insert at this point; many a time we have diverted a tantrum by joining in with it! If Tickle starts to get cross, Fairy, Husband and I all join in and stamp our feet and grumble. Within seconds, Tickle is grinning, and hamming it up for all he's worth! We usually go on for a bit, just for fun, and then either go back to what we were doing pre-tantrum, or introduce some sort of diversionary tactic that distracts him from whatever it was he was cross about in the first place. I would add a word of warning, as not all children will accept this, and some (especially older children) may think you are making fun of them, so watch very carefully for their response.

Responding in a playful way doesn't always feel like the natural thing to do, and for a long time Husband and I were stuck in the calm-accepting-empathetic response in an attempt to try and smooth things over and keep everyone regulated. However as we've relaxed, so has Tickle, and now diffusing situations with a bit of laughter is quite commonplace in our house. Things that work well for us in potentially difficult situations are things like Tickle having a 'race' with Mummy to see who can get dressed first, having a song that we sing when we tidy up, all choosing the same vegetable to eat from our plate, and eating it all at the same time, and even simple things like having a selection of really fun bath toys so that it's a time for play and bonding rather than a chore.

Shame

I'm going to pause a minute for a quick word about shame. Shame is a strong and debilitating emotion. If you think of guilt as the feeling of having done something bad, then shame could be described as the feeling of being intrinsically bad as a person. There is a high chance your adopted or fostered child will be extremely vulnerable to feelings of shame; they may already believe that it is their own fault they were removed from their birth parents, and perhaps believe that they are inherently 'bad' or 'naughty' children.

Parenting with PACE is one of the ways to help encourage children out of the cycle of shame. By responding playfully to them, we teach them that they are interesting and fun people to be around. We accept them as they are, and we empathise with what they have been through. There is no blame attached to actions, simply a curiosity to find what might be lying underneath them. Whatever the child has or hasn't done, the relationship can be repaired.

Repair is your most important tool in fighting the cycle of shame – if you can show the child that your relationship will withstand any action, any bad behaviour, that you will still love them whatever, this is a really powerful way to override the child's feeling of being a bad person at their core. When a child believes that they are a good person who sometimes makes mistakes, they have the ability to process their feelings as 'guilt' rather than shame, and the ability to learn from them. I'll expand on this a bit in the next chapter.

Grounding techniques

Another technique for managing Tickle's behaviour that has been really effective in our house is the use of grounding techniques. If you have a child with special needs you may know this as a 'sensory diet'. Grounding techniques can be anything that makes use of the senses, the idea being that awareness of sensory input can bring a dissociated child back to the present and to awareness of their bodies, not trapped in the past in their traumatic thoughts.

In our family we most often use grounding techniques in a preventative way, but we have also used them to help Tickle bring himself back from traumatic memories. There was a time when Tickle was dissociating very frequently and quite severely, and the only thing that would help was holding him firmly until he'd calmed down. It took a long time though, and it was emotionally very draining. For some children this wouldn't work at all, especially if they are triggered by physical contact, so you would need to find another way of introducing the sensory input – maybe through loud music, a weighted blanket, nice smells, etc. I would recommend experimenting with a few different things to see what works for you.

As Tickle is fairly able verbally, it often works well for us to ask him what he can *see* or *hear* in the room around him. Describing his environment can help bring him back to the present moment – and it requires him to use his 'human' brain, in effect forcing him to override his amygdala and fight/flight response. Sometimes we use verbal prompts to remind him that he is at our house, that this is his 'safe' house. Usually I will be gently squeezing his hand or arm as I'm talking to him, or hugging him close to me. Sometimes I speak really quietly right up close to his ear. Often I sing to him, and jiggle him up and down, or tap his knees or hands in time. Sometimes giving him something to eat or drink works wonders. (Other times he'll just throw it across the room.)

Wrapping him in a soft blanket and rocking him while we sing nursery rhymes is the current favourite, but he also likes a squeeze (a firm hug), and having nice-smelling cream rubbed in to his hands. This has the added benefit of being a great bonding exercise between us.

We have a sensory kit for Tickle, made up of various items such as juggling scarves, squeezy toys, balls that light up, beanbags, fiddle toys etc. The kit lives at school, and works pretty well if it's introduced when Tickle's arousal is fairly low. If you catch him at the right time the sensory kit can head off a meltdown completely – although if you're too late you might find it being thrown at the nearest wall!

Music is another thing that can work well for soothing Tickle. I sing to him a lot, but for older kids, you could try asking them to make themselves a playlist of songs that they can listen to when they're feeling down.

This might sound silly, but taking deep breaths also works pretty well with Tickle. Sometimes Husband will sit and breathe with him, and the deliberate motion and extra oxygen does seem to work wonders.

Giving up the battle

Back in the self-care chapter I wrote a little about choosing your battles, or defining your behaviour zones. In the context of this chapter, I also want to mention the benefits of giving up completely. Sometimes the rules that we impose on ourselves and our children are completely arbitrary, or have been inherited from other people, perhaps our parents, and don't really make sense in the context of our own lives.

For example, a while ago Tickle seemed to decide that 5.00am was the best time of day to be getting up and out of bed. Naturally, he wasn't impressed by the fact that we would rather be asleep at that time, and made his feelings quite clear in a loud voice. We started off trying to persuade him to go back to sleep, but he would lie in his bed and scream. Then we said OK, he could get up and play, as long as he stayed quietly in his bedroom. But of course, unavailable caregivers are a big trigger for Tickle, so that didn't work either – instead of lying in his bed screaming, he'd stand next to ours and scream.

Mornings became a huge battle for control, and everyone was exhausted.

So we decided to give up. And it felt great.

When we thought about it we realised that all the 'rules' we had been trying to enforce were totally arbitrary. Tickle can't go downstairs until six o'clock – why not? What difference does it actually make?

After this, when Tickle would wake at 5.00am Husband would get him a drink and snack, if he wanted it, and leave him to play. We snoozed. Then if Tickle wanted the iPad to watch CBeebies, we give it to him. We snooze. Then if he wants to go downstairs and play, we let him. We snooze. He sometimes sounds like he's getting a bit silly, so we call down and remind him he'd have to come up if he was going to be silly. He calms down. We snooze.

On the whole, this works pretty well for us. There are still good and bad days, and sometimes Husband will snooze on the sofa rather than in bed, but giving up on the idea that we have to impart rules like 'You can't have the iPad before 6.00am' has made our life immeasurably easier.

Choice

This leads me on to something else which can be incredibly powerful – choice. Adopted and fostered children find themselves in a situation where they have no control over anything that happens to them. Big, life-changing decisions are made *for* them, by adults. Often they can react back by *having* to be in control of everything – either because that is the way they have learnt to survive, or because they feel so powerless that they will do anything to claw back a bit of independence.

I believe it is important to give our children an element of choice. This goes from picking what they want for dinner, to choosing when to hug and not to hug, to being asked to take responsibility for their behaviour.

When Tickle is feeling unsafe, he can be contrary and deliberately provocative. He will try to do things that he knows are silly, or are not allowed, so that I will tell him off or stop him from doing them. He's trying to provoke conflict because that is what his previous experience of parenting is. Obviously I'm not going to let him do anything that means he'll seriously injure himself, but I have found that if I give him the choice he can sometimes be capable of making a sensible decision. For example, instead of saying 'Tickle, don't dive head-first off the bed' I might ask him what he thinks could happen if he were to do that, and if he still thinks it's a good idea.

I find that I have to be in a good place mentally to be able to really put this in to practice. On days when I'm stressed out, and Tickle is playing up, my instinct is to try and take control of the situation. But the more I try to take control, the more Tickle resists it. The trouble is, then we're locked in a power struggle, and it's no longer about the relationship, building security, or supporting Tickle, it's about getting him to do what I want him to do. There may be times when this is completely appropriate (for example, when I don't want him to put his hand on a hot stove) but for the most part this struggle is unnecessary.

A couple of days ago, Tickle asked to touch my glitter lamp, and I said no because it's hot. He got that slight crazed look in his eye and said 'I'm going to touch this!' I said 'OK, if you want to. It is hot though, so you might hurt yourself.' Sure enough, he touched it, and sure enough, it was hot. Obviously I wasn't going to let him *really* hurt himself, but he is much more likely to change his behaviour because he remembers that my glitter lamp is uncomfortably hot than because we've had a 20-minute fight over whether he's allowed to touch it or not. Using this approach over time, two things will happen – firstly, he'll learn that Mummy does actually know best sometimes, and that if I say things are not suitable for touching then I'm probably right, and secondly, he will make *his own* behaviour choices based on his experiences.

Limiting choice

It might sound like a complete contradiction, but at times it is necessary to *limit* the choices Tickle has if his behaviour is starting to become confrontational or he is spiralling out of control. For example, at 5.20am this morning Tickle decided he wanted to go downstairs to play, but given all the shouting and banging that had occurred so far this morning we didn't think it was a brilliant idea. We gave Tickle a choice of playing in his bedroom, or coming to sit with us so we could help him to calm down. It became apparent fairly quickly that he didn't approve of either of those options, and he hit, kicked, and bit me.

When Tickle escalates into violence, then I take his choice away. I explained to him that as he had hit, kicked, and bitten me, it seemed to me that he was not able to make the decision that I had offered him for himself. For that reason, I was going to make the decision for him, and I was of the opinion that he needed some help to calm down. (I am paraphrasing slightly, it came out as much more of a crazed yelp.) On this particular occasion, Husband was in need of sleep, so I took Tickle back to his room, put on some music, put him back in to bed and held his hands. I am making it all sound much more straightforward than it was in practice, but I think the reality is that I have got so used to parenting in this way that I almost do it without thinking. You *have* to be consistent – kind, but consistent. Tickle knows that if I say he has to sit with me for two minutes then nothing else is going to happen until he has done that. Even then he still fights against it, but in some ways he *has* to fight against it, to find out whether I really mean it or not. All children do this, but adopted and fostered children even more so, because they have often had such inconsistent care they just don't know what to expect. Children need to know where the boundaries are, and they absolutely will fight against them – *because that's the only way they can be sure that it is a definite boundary*, and that you will stick to it.

Attachment

As I mentioned before, repair is a key tool when it comes to surviving challenging behaviours. Everything, absolutely everything, is built on the foundation of a solid relationship between you and your child.

Attachment is a term that is used a lot in adoption and fostering circles, but one that is widely misunderstood. Attachment is important, it's the basis from which your child will learn to regulate their emotions, but the way it is often talked about in the context of adoption is unhelpful at best, and at worst completely misleading.

In the next chapter I'm going to take you through a whistle-stop tour of attachment; from the basics of the theory, to how it's relevant to you, and even looking at some alternative suggestions for the language that we use in adoption and fostering. But first, a little story about my daughter...

From the blog

Fairy's Story

Fairy was only 5 when we started the adoption process. We did what we could to prepare her, as you do, and being the beautiful, empathetic child that she is, she really got it. She instinctively understood about her future brother being worried, about having to teach him that we are kind, that we would look after him. That it would take a while for him to settle in. Throughout the process, both Husband and I, and various social workers periodically used to ask her if she had any questions, but she only ever had the one: 'How long will it take for us to get to know each other?'

She knew it was a question that couldn't be answered, obviously, but regardless, that was the thing she most wanted to know, and she held it clutched to her chest like a talisman.

Fast-forward four years, and she and I were chatting about this in the car, part way through our half-term break. Little things have been shifting this week; like the way she puts herself in charge of getting his drink, or the way she lets him follow her around for a bit while she's building a bug house, rearranging all the bits of moss that he's put in the wrong place.

As we were talking, it occurred to me that, had I got pregnant and had another baby, it probably would have taken at least the same amount of time for them to form a meaningful relationship – but it wouldn't have seemed odd, because for most of that time the baby would pretty much just have been pooing, sleeping, or eating. The baby would have spent time just being a baby, and Fairy would have been able to use that time to make her own adjustments, realign her world a bit, and figure out where her place is now she has to share her mum.

But instead of all that, her baby brother came fully formed, with a loud voice, and five and a half years of abuse and neglect. He has needs far greater than anyone ever suspected – including his social worker, who admitted as much to me at a LAC review about nine months in.

Babies are hard work, I'm not going to deny that. But instead of snuggles and DVDs while I was feeding on the sofa, Fairy sat in her room listening to Tickle rage and scream at me, while I was holding him on the sofa, to stop him from hitting me. There were no nap times, when Fairy and I could have had some special time. There was no stream of relatives eager to take the baby off for a cuddle, or push it round the block in a stroller. Instead, Tickle infiltrated every waking moment, demanding as much from her as he does from me and Husband, because he doesn't really understand the difference between a sister and a parent.

It's that weird thing again, where adoptive parents say something, and biological parents say it's normal, and all kids do that. Like, I might say, Tickle wants Fairy to look after him. That sounds pretty normal, right? But if I were to explain that Tickle thinks Fairy can take him to his swimming lesson, which is a 25-minute drive away.... sounds a bit less normal now. He genuinely doesn't seem to understand that there's a difference between Fairy being the one who can get him a drink, and Fairy being the one who can take him to soft play.

So I have spent the last few days trying not to get too excited, and have quietly watched from afar with butterflies in my stomach and tears threatening, as Fairy has cautiously tried on her big sister role. They have played together three days in a row, with no hitting, no crying, and only one disagreement, in which Fairy came out on top – just. I could sense she was about to crumble; Tickle was wanting to do something with one of her toys, and kept arguing back when she said no, and then just on the point where the wobble came in to her voice, and I was about to intervene, Tickle gave in – just like that – and they carried on playing. Magic.

5 Attachment

Attachment is a fashionable word in adoption at the moment, and it's often bandied around without much care and attention. There's a lot of misunderstanding around the subject; during my adoption journey I have met social workers who dismiss attachment theory as something akin to 'pop psychology', something they *have* to teach in the preparation groups but which isn't actually that useful in real life, and equally, others who hang on to it like a life raft.

For anyone like my Husband, who has been baffled by all of this information, which seems important but isn't really making any sense, in this chapter I'm going to try to explain attachment theory, and – more importantly – how it's relevant to you and your adopted child.

In order to do this properly I want to start at the beginning, with some of the background and history of attachment theory. It might seem a bit unnecessary at first but bear with me.

What *is* attachment anyway?

Attachment refers to the relationship that a child has with a caregiver. It can be a descriptive term which refers to the quality of the relationship (e.g. a secure attachment) or it can simply indicate that there is a dependent relationship present. Virtually every single person on this planet will have attachments to at least one person, most likely more than one. Having a relationship with a caregiver is one of the things that keeps us alive as young babies; when we're unable to look after ourselves it's important that we can identify the people most likely to take care of us.[15]

Attachment doesn't have to be between a baby and an adult – it can describe any sort of dependent relationship, whether it's between siblings, grandparents and grandchildren, childminders, foster carers etc. It's not based (entirely) on physical dependence, and it's not as simple as loving the person who feeds you; it's about emotional dependence, support, the need to feel safe and secure, etc. Forming attachments as infants helps us with the development of our self-confidence, the ability to regulate our emotions, forming relationships with others, the ability to empathise, and much more.

Attachment is a very basic term for a very basic relationship: it does not attempt to describe the complexities of the relationship, just to acknowledge that there is one there. Sometimes people talk about 'improving' attachment, which is a bit of a misnomer, in my opinion. You can't improve an attachment because attachment is a description of a collection of behaviours. It's like saying you can improve yellow. You can display more of one type of behaviour, change the level of connection, or the quality of the relationship, which may lead to a different sort of attachment – like adding in a bit of red to make orange. You may find you have improved quality of life, level of satisfaction from the relationship, etc, etc, but you haven't improved the yellow to make it orange, you've just changed it slightly. I usually prefer to say something like 'Jack is showing secure attachment behaviours much more frequently these days'. It's more accurate, and it's usually what people mean by 'improving' anyway.

The background of attachment theory

One of the things that's important to remember when thinking about psychology is that it's all about people – feelings, emotions, behaviours, thoughts – and because of that it's virtually impossible to ever get a definitive answer on anything. All we can really do is observe, speculate, and try out some different theories to see what fits best. That's all it is when you hear people talk about attachment – a theory.

In the late 60s and early 70s there were a lot of developmental psychologists working on attachment and early relationships. One of these was Mary Ainsworth, who devised an experiment which has had a huge influence on how we think about different types of attachment today, particularly in the context that it is used relating to adoption.

In her famous 'Strange Situation'[16] experiment, Ainsworth and her colleagues invited mothers and young children in to their lab. They had devised a 'situation' which would be novel for the children – it started with the child playing in a strange room, then an unknown person entering the room, the child's mother leaving (so the child was alone with the stranger), and then the mother coming back. They wanted to see how the children would react in a new situation, and in particular how they related to their mother during that time.

It may be worth bearing in mind that these children weren't 'diagnosed' with attachment of a particular type; the attachment styles which you may have heard talked about today were developed and defined by simply observing the behaviour of the children in the study, and looking for patterns and similarities between them. In other words, the behaviour came first, and this led to the development of the theory.

The other thing you might wish to ponder over as you're reading this, is that the attachment relationships observed as part of the study were specific to each particular infant-caregiver pairing; in other words, it may have been observed that a child had a secure attachment to their mother during the study, but you can't automatically generalise as to whether or not that child would have displayed the same behaviours with a different caregiver. (This is in fact why only mothers were used in the study – so that the researchers could be as sure as they could that any differences they observed were down to attachment styles, rather than the fact that the children were with different family members.)

During the adoption process I have heard children described as having a 'secure attachment style'. However, when you use the term 'attachment' you are describing a set of behaviours which embody the relationship a child has *with a particular caregiver*, and therefore it is possible (and normal) for a child to have a different quality of attachment relationship with different adults. You could say, for example, that a child has a secure attachment to their mother, and an insecure attachment to their father. Our therapist says it's more appropriate to talk about using 'attachment strategies', in other words, patterns of behaviour that relate to certain styles of attachment. It's a small difference, but it means that you're not labelling the child as only ever being able to display one type of attachment behaviour.

In the Strange Situation experiment, Ainsworth found that the vast majority of the children displayed a very similar set of behaviours, which she grouped together and termed 'secure' attachment behaviours. These children were happy to explore the strange environment, provided their mother was nearby to act as a 'safe base'. The children were wary of the stranger (although happy to interact with them when their mother was in the room), and were distressed when their mother left, but pleased to see her when she came back. On the mothers' return they were able to successfully comfort the child. This is generally accepted to be a fairly healthy relationship; a wariness in new situations and when meeting new people is normal, and useful in an evolutionary sense, but the important thing in this situation is that the child is reassured by the mother's presence, and is happy to explore the new environment with her nearby. Similarly with the mother leaving the room; we see the children comforted by her presence when she returns.

Around 30 percent of the children in Ainsworth's original study didn't behave as described above, and were labelled as having an 'insecure' attachment. Insecurely attached children could be split in to two fairly distinct groups: One group of children were generally upset by the whole situation; they were frightened of the stranger, distressed when their mother left the room, and not quite sure how to treat her when she came back – sometimes approaching her but also pushing her away. Ainsworth termed these behaviours 'insecure-ambivalent'. The other group of children were, on the whole, not that bothered by what was going on; they weren't particularly upset when their mother left the room, or interested when she came back, and were equally as happy to play with the stranger as their mother. Ainsworth described these behaviours as 'insecure-avoidant'. In a later version of the study Ainsworth added a fourth attachment type, which she called 'disorganised' – meaning there was no consistent pattern of behaviour for that child.

That's all very interesting, but what does it mean for me?

The Strange Situation experiment has been replicated an enormous number of times by different researchers, and the results that Ainsworth found have proved to be fairly standard across all of the studies. This means that we can say with a reasonable amount of confidence that the behavioural differences observed in the study are caused by the one major thing that makes each mother-child pair different – the parenting style.

I will say once again we are very firmly *in theory* here, but based on the behaviours that we have seen from children in the experiment, it is possible to speculate about some of the adult behaviours that the child is regularly exposed to.

For example, with the children displaying avoidant behaviours (not bothered) we could speculate that the children are not used to getting much response from their caregiver, so have pretty much given up trying. The fact that they are not wary of the stranger and played equally as happily with them as with their own mother could suggest that the child feels a stranger is just as likely to respond to their needs as their mother is. They didn't seem upset when their mother left the room, or when she came back; perhaps they are used to spending a lot of time playing on their own.

For children displaying ambivalent behaviours (going from one extreme to another); perhaps they are not getting a consistent response from their caregivers – sometimes it may be warm and loving and at other times cold and rejecting. This is likely to make them quite anxious about approaching their caregiver, as they genuinely have no idea how they are going to react, which could explain why they cling to them one minute and try and push them away the next. They are very frightened of the stranger; perhaps they have learnt that people are unpredictable, and are not sure what the stranger might do or say.

As adoptive parents, we're often playing detective, unpicking the clues that our children drop about their former lives, and piecing them together with what we have learnt from our social workers. I believe that an understanding of the basics of attachment theory can help us delve a bit deeper, and start to imagine what sort of relationship our child may have had with their birth parents, and therefore what they are likely to expect from us. It might help us to look past a child who is supposedly 'coping' and investigate what is actually going on for them.

In our case, there are some things about Tickle's behaviour that I find really striking. Tickle goes to a local special needs school, so there is a high proportion of adults in his class. When he first started, he was assigned an adult to work with him 1:1 every day – a different one each day so that he has a chance to get to know them all. You might expect this to have been overwhelming for Tickle, but in fact from Day 1 he was perfectly happy to wander off with a virtual stranger each morning.

Looking at the attachment behaviours above, this is classic for the insecure avoidant group. From this I would guess that Tickle had been used to a fairly non-responsive caregiver, which would explain why he jumps at the chance to have a chat with anyone who seems receptive to him. However, two years down the line I have noticed a change in this behaviour, and he now definitely has his preferred adult in the class. Given the choice he would be with her 1:1 every day, and on the days when she has some office time instead of being in class he can get quite cross.

Tickle also used to change his mind a lot about whether he wanted me or Husband:

'I don't want to play with Daddy!'

'OK, I'll go away...'

'NO! I want you to play with me!'

This is often seen with the ambivalent attachment style, and suggests inconsistent responses from a caregiver – for example, sitting to watch TV, leaving Tickle to play by himself, and then occasionally grabbing Tickle and try to hug him and fuss over him.

Disorganised attachment

Above, I have described different situations where Tickle shows different attachment behaviours. This is indicative of a disorganised attachment: in other words, Tickle wasn't showing any consistent pattern of responses to a caregiver. Sometimes he was distant, sometimes he was clingy, sometimes he didn't really know who his caregiver was supposed to be.

The good news is that this has changed significantly with time, and he now shows a lot of secure attachment behaviours. He will go and play on the slide at the park as long as he knows that I'm there. He comes to me for comfort, and seeks out affection. He is less likely to strike up a conversation with a stranger in the queue at Sainsbury's, and more likely to ask me what they are having for dinner, instead of asking them directly. When he's frightened or worried he seeks me out, and asks for a cuddle.

The less good news is that disorganised attachment makes you more vulnerable to being affected by trauma. According to Dan Siegel, you're also more likely to be predisposed to dissociative episodes,[17] as I described in chapter 1.

Attachment as protection

Attachment is what we call a *protective factor* in determining how someone will react to trauma. The attachment behaviours themselves aren't the trauma, in fact quite the opposite – they are the ways of behaving that have best served the child to help them survive in their environment. If you have a caregiver who consistently ignores you, of course you will withdraw from them to protect yourself from continually getting hurt. The problem arises when the child is moved to a new environment where that level of protection is no longer needed, and the previous behaviours which have worked to keep the child safe now cause problems.

If you have a secure attachment with *any* adult, even if they are not your main caregiver, it will give you some form of (emotional) protection when it comes to dealing with the effects of trauma. The trouble is, a lot of adopted children have not had a safe adult in their lives, and are left vulnerable. Without some form of social support, children cannot learn to regulate emotions. The very act of co-regulating (being comforted) with an adult creates the pathways in the brain which allow the child to regulate themselves when they are away from the caregiver[18]. In other words, your brain is practising emotional regulation with someone who already knows how to do it, and when it's ready it can have a go by itself. Attachment is the bedrock from which that can happen.

'Attachment issues'

Now there's a phrase which is a little overused. 'This adopted child has attachment issues.' Of course they do. They have been removed from their primary attachment figure, and handed to a stranger. They don't know who is going to feed them, where they are allowed to sleep, whether they are safe... But gradually they work out where they are in their new world, and they form new attachments. They can't help it – it's instinctive, it's a built-in survival mechanism.

In the original Strange Situation experiment, Ainsworth classified around 30 percent of the children as insecurely attached, a figure that has been found to be consistent in further experiments. I very much doubt that those 30 percent were all adopted children, and only adopted children, in every iteration of this study over the decades; therefore we must conclude that biological children, at home with their biological parents, and living a life normal enough not to be deemed unsafe by the child protection authorities, can also have insecure attachments. By the definition above, these children also qualify as having 'attachment issues', and yet, do they display the same behaviour patterns as our adopted children?

Let's look at this from another angle. Tickle is displaying signs of having a secure attachment to me. He gets upset when I go away, he is happy when I come back. If something scares him, he takes comfort from being physically near to me. He prefers to be with me over strangers. He's reasonably happy to explore new environments with my help, but he does like to know where I am, and will come back to me every now and again to check in, make sure I have seen his latest descent down the slide, and so on.

So, if you subscribe to the 'attachment issues' theory, you would assume that Tickle should now be fine, correct?

The truth is that Tickle is very far from fine. And this is really my point – by simplifying everything to 'attachment issues' we are actually losing sight of some of the important things that are causing problems for our adopted children.

If we are going to have any chance at all of helping Tickle, and thousands of others like him, we must stop using 'attachment' as an excuse, and make an effort to properly understand what it means.

Don't misunderstand me – attachment is a real issue. But it is being used as an excuse for not digging deeper. An excuse for not helping him *('Well of* course *he's going to find it difficult to behave, because, you know, attachment...').* An excuse for not helping parents *('You just need to build your attachment...').* An excuse for lazy advice from professionals who have jumped on the attachment bandwagon without bothering to understand it first. An excuse to not carry out a thorough assessment of need (because he has 'attachment issues' and that explains everything), an excuse not try to understand what is *really* going on. *It has become the hook on which to hang every problem that adopted children have.*

Here's the bottom line: secure attachments help children feel safe. They help children learn to regulate their emotions, to understand the world, to explore their sense of self. Early attachments can form the blueprints for future relationships. Building a secure attachment relationship with your adopted child is very important, and will help with having a strong foundation from which they can begin to explore their trauma. The attachment is not the end goal, but a basis from which the child can begin to explore and work through their trauma.

So what do I *do* about it?

Frustratingly, there's probably not an awful lot you can do that you aren't already doing. Attachment is not something that you make a decision to do, it is instinctive, and it is survival-driven. All of the behaviours that your child exhibits have developed because they gave your child the best chance of survival in the environment they were in. If a child is continually and painfully rejected by a caregiver, the only thing they can do to protect themselves from the pain is to stop depending on the caregiver.

I have found that understanding where these behaviours come from plays a big part in helping me to accept them, as well as enabling me to look at ways that I can adjust *my* behaviour in order to help Tickle understand that Husband and I aren't going to treat him in the same way his birth parents did.

As I answer the question 'Where are we going?' for the 67th time on the 15-minute journey to school, that we make on five days out of every seven, I will try to remember that the adults of Tickle's past life didn't spend time interacting with him. As he tells me to go away but screams at me when I do, I will try to remember that Tickle is probably trying to reject me before I get a chance to reject him, but is simultaneously terrified of that actually happening. As he screams 'TALK TO ME!' when I am taking three minutes out from our game to ask Fairy how her day at school went, I will try to remember that Tickle may have *had* to scream in order to get attention in the past.

Thinking beyond attachment

As I have said, attachment is a really important part of healing our children, but it's not the be all and end all. Attachment is the foundation from which trauma can be healed, but when you are trying to understand a child's behaviour, it's useful to keep a few other concepts in mind.

Shame

I touched on shame briefly in the last chapter, and I want to come back to it now in a bit more detail. Many people might use 'guilt' and 'shame' interchangeably, but from a psychological point of view it is useful to see them as two separate things. There have been many articles, formal and informal about the subject, but one I particularly like is by Joseph Burgo in the 'Psychology Today' magazine[19] where he describes shame as an emotion that relates to how you feel about yourself, whereas guilt involves an awareness of the impact that our actions have had on other people.

The psychologist Lawrence Kohlberg devised a theory of moral development[20], which is interesting to consider in this context. Kohlberg believed that our moral development happened in stages, and that our moral judgement and reasoning changed and developed over time. The bit that particularly interests me when thinking about shame is Kohlberg's Level 1: Pre-conventional morality. Kohlberg theorised that children up to the age of nine haven't yet developed their own internal moral code, instead rely on taking cues from adults around them. In other words, the child does not have the ability to make a judgement on right and wrong based on their own feelings, only on what they have observed or learnt from adults around them. (It is worth noting that Kohlberg's stages model has come in for criticism, in particular the linking of ages to each separate stage, however it does provide an interesting springboard for discussion.)

Kohlberg's Level 1 is further split in to two stages, the first of which is known as 'Obedience and punishment orientation'. In this first stage, Kohlberg believes that a child's motivation for good behaviour is solely to avoid punishment. This is something I see a *lot* in Tickle. If I ask him to do something his reflexive response is 'What will happen?'. Sometimes he will say 'If I hit you will you hit me back?' or 'If I bite you will you go away?' He is trying to understand how his actions relate to a response from me, and struggles to understand if I try to explain that we don't hit people because it's not kind. I have lost count of the number of times that I have said 'We don't hit people' only for him to respond 'Why not? What will happen?'

If it is true that young children rely on adults for moral judgements, then adopted and fostered children are likely to have learnt – and internalised – some negative and unhelpful ideas about themselves, other people, and right and wrong in general. Perhaps they have been told off for wetting themselves, for crying, or for making a noise. In Tickle's case, I have had to repeat over and over that adults are not allowed to hurt children. This is not something he instinctively understands, so I have had to be explicit.

In summary, a child will look to adults for guidance on what is right and what is wrong. When an adult shouts at, or tells off a child, this produces an uncomfortable feeling inside, that we know as shame. Being told off is not nice, and the child will feel distressed. They may feel that they have let their parents down. This process is important for developing socially acceptable behaviour, and understanding risks in our environment. In a relationship where there is a positive, secure attachment, the child will turn to the parent for comfort, and through receiving this will be reassured that, as Dan Hughes says, 'the person and the relationship are more important than any action that either of them has taken.'[21] In other words, they are still loved, regardless of whatever they did to make their parents cross.

Self-regulation starts at a very basic level; the child doesn't like being shouted at, so they try not to do the thing which prompted the shouting. Over time, they begin to understand that their actions have an effect on other people, so instead of feeling shame ('I have been told off because I am a bad person') they can feel guilt ('I have been told off because I hit my sister and made her cry'). This difference is important – the difference between *doing* something bad, and *being* a bad person.

Imagine growing up in an abusive environment, being 'punished' constantly but not understanding why, and never having a chance to make up with the person you have upset. Do you think you might grow up with a feeling like you are simply a 'bad person'? How might this impact on your behaviour at home, at school? Imagine if, every time you made a small mistake, got something wrong, or didn't understand something, this simply fuelled your belief that you are worthless.

When Tickle first came to live with us he would get extremely angry if he said something wrong or made a mistake. I now recognise that this would have reinforced his feeling of shame. The good news is that over time this has changed significantly, and he is now even able to laugh at himself – 'What am I like?!' he will chuckle!

The self-concept

Following on from the above, we can now start to consider the self-concept, or in other words, a child's idea of his or herself as a person. If you have grown up with an ingrained sense of shame, how might that affect the development of your self-concept? How might you see yourself as different from other children, and how could this affect the way you behave around them?

Even more important for adopted children, how would it then feel to be placed in a new family and to be told that everything you have believed about yourself is totally wrong?

Absolutely crucial to the development of the self-concept is the chance to interact with the world around us, and the gathering of feedback from those interactions. The child first develops a sense of themselves as a separate being to everything around them, and realise that they (as with other objects in the world) have properties that differ from other things. As they grow, children begin to define things as fitting in to categories, and will start to place themselves in to categories as appropriate. Usually the first categories to be defined are age and gender.[22]

I mentioned previously a boy I worked with who was struggling in school and displaying challenging behaviour. His headteacher was convinced he was autistic; I knew he wasn't, and so did his teacher. When I reported this to the head after a few sessions her instant response was 'That's interesting. So do you think he has attachment disorder?' Disorder? No. He had a good attachment to his teacher, showing that he was capable of a secure attachment relationship. What I did think however, was that this little boy had virtually no self-concept. (Obviously there were many more issues, but in the four sessions I did with him this was the thing that was most immediately obvious.) It was a strange experience; I asked him to tell me about himself, and beyond his name and age he was totally stuck. He couldn't tell me what he liked doing, about his family set-up, where he lived, who he lived with and could only tell me about likes and dislikes by answering yes/no questions about different subjects. He was six at the time, with no identified learning needs.

One of the reasons the head thought this child was autistic was because he reacted really badly to any change of routine. But when he can't even comprehend who he *is* on a fundamental level, you can't really blame him for hanging on to the anchor of anything that represents security and constancy in his life.

Permanence

This brings us neatly on to another word which has become somewhat of a 'buzzword': permanence.

Permanence (in adoption terms) just means a child being in their forever home, whether that's with an adoptive family, long-term foster care, with relations, or safely back in their birth family.

For our children, I don't think it's that simple. For them, I believe that permanence is a feeling, deep inside, and one that may not come easily.

You can have a secure attachment to a caregiver and still not have a sense of permanence, still not *really* believe that you aren't going to move on again. Tickle still occasionally talks about the 'next' house. When we go on holiday we still have to explain that we are going back home again.

I think perhaps people in adoption are sometimes thinking about permanence when they talk about attachment. For me attachment is a relationship centred around a particular person, and unique to that person. You can have an attachment to someone which will feel the same wherever you are in the world. Attachment is about growing, learning, reciprocity, give and take, interaction, and love. It grows and changes. Permanence is stability; a feeling of belonging, of certainty, of home.

Expectations

It may sound simplistic, but I believe this is an important topic, and one that is all too easy to overlook. I had a conversation with a former teacher of Tickle's, which went something like this:

Teacher: Tickle got a bit crazy and bumped in to another kid and spilled his juice.

Me: Yes, that would really upset him.

Teacher: Oh no, the juice didn't go on Tickle, just the other kid!

Me: Yes... that would really upset him.

Despite knowing Tickle's background, his teacher hadn't made the association that certain actions might cause Tickle to expect particular reactions, even if they are ones which might not be a part of his new life. To use this example, Tickle has always responded with panic whenever any food or drink gets spilled. We can only imagine what reaction his brain is expecting to follow.

Schema theory

In psychology, the idea of having certain 'expectations' about life is known as "schema theory"[23], and was developed by a cognitive psychologist called Jean Piaget. A schema is a little chunk of information that tells you about something that you might experience in your environment. For example, you might have a schema of a dog, which holds the following information: animal, four legs, tail (often wags), often has tongue hanging out, barks. This means that if you see a new type of dog that you've never seen before, you're still able to recognise it as a dog, because it fits in to your 'dog' schema. Children's schemata (plural of schema) are often fairly simplistic, which is why they sometimes miscategorise things. As they learn new information about their environment, their schemata adapt to the new information, giving them more detailed blueprints about life, the universe, and everything.

There are a couple of interesting processes relating to schema theory, which are to do with what happens when you encounter new situations.

Let's say for example that you have a schema about going to a restaurant: go in, wait at the entrance, and someone will come and show you to a table. You choose from the menu, and order at your table. You have a set of expectations which allow you to seamlessly function in any new restaurant situation; you know what's going on, what to expect, and how to react. If you were to visit a new restaurant which works in the way that you expect (based on your schema) then you'll be fine. Schema theory calls this assimilation: using an existing schema to manage new experiences.

If however the restaurant that you happen to end up in one night doesn't work in this way, then you are in a state of disequilibrium. Perhaps you're waiting for a table when the waiters expect you to order at the bar first. It's an uncomfortable feeling, so you need to adapt your schema to deal with this alternative scenario, otherwise you'll just wait at the door all night expecting to be led to a table. Once you've realised what you need to do, you can alter your behaviour, and return to a state of equilibrium. And a nice meal, hopefully.

This process of adaptation is how Piaget believes that we grow and learn. In our restaurant scenario, your schema will now have developed, perhaps to sub-categorise table service restaurants and bar service restaurants.

As always, it is important to remember that all of this is just a theory, however it's quite a useful model for describing the point I want to make. The formation of schemata happens naturally, as part of the way that children and adults develop and learn about the world. They are there to help us navigate new situations without having to work things out afresh every time, to help us predict what might happen and plan ahead, and to help us filter and deal with the huge amount of information that we take in through our senses at any given moment.

For our adopted children, schemata have been a survival tool. If they can learn to recognise the link between the spilled food and the slap that follows, then maybe they can avoid it. They may relate sounds, smells, facial expressions to certain actions or consequences that – according to their schemata – will most likely follow.

According to Piaget, when a person's experience of the world can be explained by their schemata, they are in a state of cognitive equilibrium.

('Everything's fine, I know what's going on.') When something in their external environment *can't* be explained by their schemata, this is a state of disequilibrium; uncomfortable, possibly worrying, maybe even scary. In most people (as described in the restaurant example above) adaptation of schemata follows fairly naturally, and the person is back in equilibrium. However, when our adopted children are plucked out of their home environment, absolutely everything is suddenly different. Very few, or even none of their schemata can explain what is going on in their new life.

Can you imagine how exhausting that must be? A constant state of disequilibrium. But based on what we have discussed about the formation of the self-concept, about internalising shame and believing yourself to be a bad person, adapting your schema to your new situation is going to mean completely reinventing yourself. *Everything you know to be true about the world is suddenly not tallying with what is going on around you.*

The closest I can get to imagine this is thinking about going to a foreign country, where I don't know the language, how the money works, what any of the food is, or how the transport system works. But even then, I would be doing that out of choice, with a solid self-concept, confidence in myself and my own ability to keep safe, and without having had any traumatic experiences of travelling.

In summary

I think the most appropriate way to summarise this chapter is that however you want to think about it – attachment, schema theory, self-concept – please remember that it is just a theory.

Children are individuals. They are constantly changing. Psychology has discovered certain traits, certain expected behaviours, but you are the person who knows your child the best. Take everything you know about attachment and trauma, and decide how it applies to your child.

Take the bits you need, and put aside the bits you don't. (You may need them later, mind!)

Attachment is essential to thrive in this world. Added to that it's very interesting to learn about, but don't fall in to the trap of thinking it is the magic wand that will solve all your problems. What it definitely will do is give you a solid base to build on.

From the blog

Mornings

Tickle woke up at 5.30am this morning, and shouted at us because he wasn't allowed to go downstairs. We explained he had the choice of playing in his bedroom or going back to bed. He eventually chose to play. Five minutes later he was back and we repeated the whole thing again. He went off. Five minutes later he had reached the point where he couldn't bear to be alone for one more second so he came in and said he wanted a cuddle.

He climbed in to bed next to me, and I put my arms around him. He lifted up one hand, and smacked me round the face. I kept cuddling him, but held on to both his hands so he couldn't hit me. I told him he's not allowed to hit, and that I was feeling cross and sad. He's only allowed to stay in bed if he can be calm. He said he would be, but soon was cackling and laughing, chattering nonsense at the top of his voice.

I took him back to his bedroom and sat on the bed holding him on my lap. He headbutted me on the shoulder. (I'm giving you the edited highlights here, in reality there was quite a lot more shouting than this.)

A few minutes later it all suddenly left him and his body went limp. He was concerned about me, because he doesn't like me to be sad. I told him I was sad because he hit me. 'Oh dear.' he said. 'That wasn't good choices.' I agreed. He said sorry, and showed me how to sign it as well. Then he lifted up his top and asked me to tickle his tummy, which made me smile. 'You're happy now!' he said, delighted.

'I love you very much' he said. 'I love you, I hit you.'

'I'm not sure what you mean?' I said.

'I love you, and I hit you.'

'Do you mean you still love me even though you hit me?'

'Yes! I still love you, even though I hit you.

[pause]

I didn't mean to.'

'I know, darling. I know you didn't mean to.'

6 Disclosures

This was a hard chapter to write, and I suspect it's not going to be much fun to read either. In addition to the subject matter, there was a difficult balance to strike between needing to tell *my* story, and doing it without betraying Tickle's confidence. I worry a little that I have already said too much. For that reason I haven't explicitly talked about his disclosures or repeated what he said, but if you think you may be triggered by the subject matter it may still be best to skip to the next chapter. In any case, this might be a good time to stop reading for a minute and get yourself a cup of tea – remember your self-care!

In this chapter I have written as candidly as I can about what it's like when your child tells you they have been abused. I am hoping to provide some sort of guidance for anyone who may find themselves in my situation in the future, as when it happened to me I had no idea what to do. I asked for help, information, for books to read to give me ideas on how to manage disclosures, and was told there was nothing. If you are reading this in the same situation as I was, feeling as desperate and alone as I felt, I want to be able to pass on a virtual hug, and a few coping strategies I've learnt along the way. I've done my best to balance it out, but please forgive me if this chapter is a bit vague in some areas, and just know that I am trying to leave Tickle's story for him to tell if and when he decides.

Tickle had only been with us about six weeks when he made his first disclosure. I can remember it really well in some ways; I remember we were sitting on the floor of the bathroom, I remember the feel of the towel I had wrapped around him, I remember the feeling that this was the climax of a massive screaming meltdown. I don't remember exactly what he said. It's written down, in the back of the green book that I was using to make all my adoption-related notes from meetings. I could go and look it up, but I prefer not to look in there if I can help it. There's quite a lot written in the back these days.

That first time, sat on the bathroom floor, the disclosure wasn't a big surprise, as we knew that Tickle's birth parent had physically abused his older sibling, and that they had admitted to giving Tickle a 'tap' once or twice. Shortly after that, more bits started to trickle out. I don't remember too much about them, but I do remember for one incident Tickle's social worker saying, 'Oh yes, [his sibling] was adamant that this had happened, they must have been telling the truth!' (At the time I was too numb to really register anything apart from 'Yes, they are believing us', but looking back now there are so many things I find wrong with this.)

Gradually, more things began to come out as Tickle's language and understanding improved. I often felt like he was trying to tell me something but didn't quite have the right words, or he couldn't quite make sense of what he was remembering. Then, weeks or months later, it would suddenly come out and I'd realise this was what he had been trying to tell me all along.

Bath times were initially very traumatic for Tickle, and it wasn't too long before he was able to tell us why. (In fact, most of his initial disclosures happened in the bathroom.) By this point Tickle understood the difference between 'accident' and 'on purpose' and was very clear that the incident he described was 'on purpose'. It's not for me to say whether it was or not, but that was Tickle's understanding of the situation.

I originally trained as a teacher, and then worked in a variety of jobs necessitating child protection training, so I had a fairly good idea how to handle disclosures at work: reassure the child and then go and get someone else to deal with it. Write down what they said. Pass it on, pass it up the chain.

However, here at home there is no chain. I told Tickle's social worker, obviously, and she wrote it down as well, but that was it. I asked whether I should discourage him from saying anything more (as per my professional training) but no, I should encourage him to talk as we want to find out more about what he's been through.

If I hadn't had the professional training I have had, and if I hadn't happened to work for the police child protection team in my university gap year, I don't think I would have had a clue how to handle this. As it was, I still struggled, and I still made a lot of mistakes.

The first rule is this: don't put words in their mouth. Tickle has a habit of saying yes to everything, so I had to frame things carefully. He didn't have the language skills or emotional development to simply tell me everything, so I needed to ask him questions – but questions that let him give me an answer himself, rather than just agreeing with something I'd said.

In the early days, it would go something like this:

Me: Tickle, you look like you've got some funny feelings.

Tickle: YES! (Or sometimes, NO! and a continuation of whatever madness was happening at the time.)

Me: Would you like to talk about them?

T: Yes. (Or No!)

Me: I wonder if you feel sad/cross/worried/frightened etc.

T: [picks one of the above]

Me: I wonder if you are feeling sad/cross/worried about something in this house or are you remembering something from another house?

T: Another house.

Me: I wonder if it was Foster Carers' house, or Birth Parents' house?

T: Birth Parents' house.

Me: OK so you're worried about something that you are remembering from when you lived at Birth Parents' house, have I got that right or is that not right?

T: Right.

Me: I wonder what might have happened at Birth Parents' house to make you feel worried?

This was the point I couldn't really lead him any more, so just had to wait until he was ready to tell me something. Sometimes he did, sometimes he said he didn't know, and I just reassured him that he was safe here, and he could tell me whenever he was ready. 'It's OK to be worried' became our mantra. It was important to help him understand he could sit with uncomfortable feelings without feeling under pressure to tell me things.

It took me quite a long time to work that one out, if I'm honest, but it's important that your child knows that it's OK to experience these feelings. The acknowledgement and acceptance of the feeling is probably more important for them than the disclosure itself.

'Dikka-fult' feelings

The above script developed over many weeks and months, and sometimes we didn't get very far through it at all before he started screaming. It took consistent, gentle persistence to get to the point where he was disclosing anything in any detail. We encouraged him to talk by saying that it could help make his 'big feelings' a bit smaller. Again, this is something we repeated daily to him for months.

As time went on, I started to recognise the signs that were leading up to a disclosure. Tickle's behaviour would escalate, sometimes over days or weeks. I would be reciting the above script almost every day, waiting to see if he was ready to talk. Sometimes he surprised me; once he got into bed and said 'Mummy I have got funny feelings and they're sad feelings about a different house and it is Birth Parents' house.' That was a lovely moment, in a funny sort of way; it reassured me that I was on the right lines, and even if Tickle wasn't ready to talk I was at least laying the pathways for him to be able to. To me, it felt like my questions were acting as signposts for him to start to untangle what was going on in his head.

Everything Tickle told me, I wrote down, and told his social worker. I tried to get as much detail as I could each time, but sometimes it was too much and Tickle clammed up, or he couldn't work out how to answer my questions. Other times he would try, but I wouldn't understand what he'd said. Sometimes I would make mistakes, and accidentally ask a leading question about his Birth Parent (i.e. he says 'someone hurt me' and I say 'was it Birth Parent?'). I was honest about this as well – wrote it down exactly as I said it, so that if it was ever needed for evidence it was clear about which bits had come straight from Tickle and where I had led him. After that I adopted the phrase 'Do you want to tell me about that?' as a way of trying to be more open ended. So, for example, if he said it was Daddy, rather than saying 'Do you mean Birth Dad?' I would say (using 'Daddy-first name' for both) 'Do you mean Birth Dad or Husband?'

Sometimes Tickle gets mixed up, and tells me things that couldn't possibly be true. I think it can be a bit of a defence mechanism when things get too difficult to talk about. This is usually accompanied by a change in state – his voice gets higher pitched, he starts to act a bit silly. (This is usually what it looks like when Tickle is so frightened that The Monster needs to take over.) At this point I would say something like 'It seems like this might be too difficult to talk about at the moment. Shall we go to sleep now? Or talk about something else?' Over time he picked up the phrase and would tell me it was 'too dikka-fult' to talk.

I always made sure to sympathise over his 'dikka-fult' feelings, to say how sorry I was that he had to have such big feelings when he only had a small body to hold them in. Sometimes I would pretend to take them out of his tummy one by one; I'd hold it up and he would say which feeling it was, then I'd put it in my pocket and say I was looking after it. Sometimes it would be the other way round, and I would 'guess' a feeling and he would either say yes he had that feeling or no he didn't, or sometimes he would hit his pillow for each feeling that he had. Sometimes we'd get to a particular feeling and he'd hit the pillow three or four times in quick succession, so I'd reflect that back with something like 'Ooh it looks like you've got *lots* of worried/scared/sad feelings today!'

Other times I would ask Tickle to tell me what colour his feelings were. This was usually something I fell back on when it was difficult for him to talk and The Monster was out – having something concrete to focus on seems to bring Tickle back to himself, helping him override the fight/flight response and come back to his human brain. Other questions I use for this included asking where the feelings are in his body, whether they are moving around or staying in one place, whether they are fizzy, bubbly, or still, whether they are hot or cold, and so on. Sometimes I can use this technique to head off a meltdown before it escalates, by asking Tickle questions about what he has done that day, what he has eaten, what colour things are in his bedroom, etc. All of these questions require Tickle to engage his human brain, which enables him to override the instinctive responses powered by his amygdala.

Escalation

The first summer that Tickle was with us his behaviour escalated beyond anything we'd seen before. His dissociative episodes increased; there was rarely a day when he wasn't violent towards one of us, and it was often three or four times in a day. He had started displaying behaviours that I found quite worrying – for example on one occasion he was really anxious when out in public with my mum, and he stripped all his clothes off. He'd done this at home a few times as well, and would talk about himself and his body in ways that made me uncomfortable, particularly when I was helping get him ready for bed.

These behaviours continued over a few months. I remember phoning Tickle's social worker, distraught because of what I suspected, and feeling utterly unprepared for what I anticipated lay ahead. I asked whether there were any books I could read, any courses I could do to help me prepare, or even just to give me a few hints as to what to keep an eye out for – what behaviour is normal, what is not, any safeguarding measures I could put in place. Unfortunately Tickle's social worker wasn't particularly well informed about the support available, and the best she could offer was 'You're doing a good job, just keep going.' Thankfully, Adoption Twitter came through for me and I had some really helpful chats with a few other people who'd had similar experiences.

Tickle's erratic behaviour continued at a high level of intensity all throughout that summer and in to autumn, until one morning in October, at about 5.00am, Tickle finally told me what it was all about. I don't think I'm exaggerating to say I was in shock; it's one thing suspecting what is coming, it's quite another to hear it coming out of your child's mouth. I wrote it down in my green book, feeling sick. We had a meeting with Tickle's social worker scheduled for that day, and I took the green book with me to show to her and the deputy head from Tickle's school. I didn't want to say it out loud. We tried to set out a plan for what to do next. I don't remember the rest of the day; I think I wrapped myself in a duvet and cried.

The following day brought another disclosure, even more awful than the first. There is no easy way to describe how to survive hearing the most awful things you could possibly hear from a child. I think I have a little protective box inside my head, and I just climb in there and shut the lid. My body takes over, and I do what needs doing, without feeling. Observing. Curious. Accepting. Doing the right thing. Putting Tickle first.

When the disclosures first happened, it felt important that, as well as acknowledge the things Tickle was telling me, I should also try to find out as much detailed information as I could. If you find yourself needing to do this, some phrases you might find useful could be:

Do you know what it was that hurt you?

Do you think it was a hand, or a foot, or something else?

Where on your body did it hurt?

Can you point to the bit of your body that hurt?

Did it hurt on the outside of your body or the inside?

Now some time has passed and we are further in to therapy I'm not sure that side of it is as important as I thought. The social workers and the police wanted to know what had happened, and yes, in the long term it will be beneficial to Tickle to be able to tell the story in some detail, but I think I put too much pressure on myself (and probably on Tickle) to press for information, some vital nugget that we could give the authorities that would mean his birth parent could be brought to justice.

I'm going to talk more about the police later in this chapter, and describe the practicalities of what happens after your child has made a disclosure, but for now I want to stick with the emotional side of things.

Looking after yourself

Hearing this sort of thing from your child is so incredibly draining; it's vitally important that you set aside time for yourself to deal with it. I estimate it took about a month from the initial disclosure before I felt like an actual human being again, and not just like I was walking around in a daze. It affects every part of your life. There is no way of being OK with that information. If this has happened to you, I want you to know that it's absolutely fine to *not* be fine.

More than a year on, we are still living this, although it has got easier. The problem I'm having at the moment is that I have spent so much time in my protective box that I feel like I'm in there permanently. I don't know how to get out safely – if I really allowed myself to acknowledge the horror of what Tickle has been through then I would need to cry for a week. In fact, now I think about it I did cry for a week when he first told me. These days, Tickle has grown more accustomed to talking about his feelings, and we often chat about them at bed time. I am in my box, keeping safe. Ironically, the evening after I'd written the first draft of this chapter, the big disclosure came out again, a year and a day after he told me the first time.

I have had some counselling sessions, and Tickle's therapist has suggested trying to write some of it down, or finding one friend or family member that I can talk to about it. I have managed to talk to my mum a little, but writing has been my main escape. Writing, and learning as much as I can about trauma and how to heal it. At some point I know I will need to deal with it properly, but I'm not ready yet.

Telling other people

One of my big anxieties when all this started was who to tell, and how to tell them. If my friends' children were likely to be playing with Tickle, should I tell them about the disclosures? How much do I tell my parents? Tickle's teachers?

There is no right answer to this, and you will have to do what you feel best. However, in case you are worried, as I was, about how this might impact on Tickle's friendships and peer relationships, let me reassure you that it's not as common as you might think for children to re-enact their abuse. I was in a state of near panic thinking that Fairy might be in danger, and although Tickle was physically aggressive towards her, I don't think it even occurred to him to do anything more. The closest he has come is stripping off his clothes in front of her in a moment of madness, but then I doubt he is the only little boy who has ever embarrassed his sister like that!

What I would recommend however, is supervising any play quite closely. I don't let Tickle play upstairs with other children unless Husband or I are there to supervise, and I can't, for example, pop into the shower when both the children are at home and Husband is out. (I don't attribute that entirely to Tickle's abuse however, it's just part of having an adopted child.) The same rules apply if we are playing at someone else's house – Tickle plays downstairs where he can be supervised, and not in anyone's bedroom.

Husband and I decided to make Tickle's school aware of the disclosures. Initially, it was just the head and the deputy who knew the details, but later we decided that the staff who work with Tickle on a day-to-day basis did also need to know. Tickle's anxieties often come to the fore when changing clothes, or using the toilet, both of which he needs to do regularly (with adult support) at school. Husband and I (in consultation with our therapist and the headteacher) thought it was important that school staff fully understood where Tickle's behaviour was coming from, so that they could support him through it rather than seeing it as something they needed to sanction.

The other thing to be aware of at school is topics about the body. Tickle's class is just about to start some work on private and public parts of the body, so Husband and I have had a long chat with his teacher about how to approach this with him – or even whether to approach it at all. It's not just the subject matter, but also the fact that the lessons are scheduled for just before Tickle's swimming lesson, which is already difficult enough!

Schools will have their own safeguarding policies on how to deal with disclosures, which will likely be 'don't ask questions, refer to your safeguarding lead'. You might find it helpful to have a discussion with school about anything additional you'd like them to do in your particular situation. We have requested that Tickle's school use the same sorts of phrases as we do at home if he does make a disclosure at school, such as 'Poor Tickle, that must have been really difficult. Adults are not allowed to do that to children.' This will also give the school staff a bit of confidence in dealing with the situation, don't forget it may well be something they have never experienced before.

I've not found the disclosures an easy thing to talk about with my friends or family. Partly because they are intensely private to Tickle, partly because I can't actually bring myself to say the words, and partly because I don't want to put these images and ideas into someone else's head. Most people have no experience of this type of thing, and that's a really lovely way to be. I wish I could be that innocent again, and I can't bear to be the person who takes that innocence away from someone else. And then I worry that they will feel how I feel now, and will need to find someone to talk to about it, and so the chain goes on.

One thing I have found helpful however, is discussing reported cases of abuse with my friends. There was a programme on the BBC not that long ago called 'Three Girls', about the Rochester abuse scandal, and I was really keen to know who among my friends had watched it. For me, it was a sign that they were brave enough to face the subject head on, and it helped me feel more confident that I might be able to speak about it to other people in the future.

Keeping records

There is something else Tickle has been trying to tell me for a few months now but hasn't quite been able to articulate it; he keeps repeating the same thing over and over, and I keep sympathising, saying that it wasn't his fault, grown-ups are not allowed to do that to children, it's not going to happen any more. I have taken to setting the voice record app on my phone going when Tickle says he wants to talk; when you're having a 30-minute conversation and get one significant comment in the middle of that it's difficult to remember the exact wording to write down! They are not the same as a recorded interview with the police (i.e. the police couldn't make an arrest based on them), but they, and my green book could still be used as evidence. However you decide to keep records, make sure you record the date the disclosure happened, and if possible the context, so what happened just before, how the disclosure came about, and so on.

Keep talking

That's about the best advice I can give you! It will probably take a really long time, but eventually the act of talking everything through will help Tickle to process his memories in a way that means they have less of an impact on his everyday life. If you think back to the beginning of this book when we talked about traumatic memories being stored differently – Tickle needs to store them as 'stories' that he can tell himself, rather than 'feelings' that trick him in to thinking he's right back in the memory.

Therapy has been a life line for us. Initially the social workers and the police were reluctant for us to start therapy, because they said that might affect Tickle's credibility as a witness, were this to go to trial. I don't think that is actually true, and in any case, our therapist videos every session so if there ever was a question about how therapy had affected his recollections of what happened to him, there is a record of exactly what he has said and when. Regardless of whether this is true however, our main priority was getting therapeutic help for Tickle.

Why?

The hardest question that Tickle has ever asked me is 'Why?' Why did his birth parent hurt him? Why did his mother not keep him safe? He has learnt at school that if someone hurts you, you should tell an adult, and can't understand why someone didn't do that for him.

The only answer I can really give Tickle is the honest one: 'I don't know'. On our therapist's advice, I empathise with him. 'I really wish I did know the answer Tickle, because I can see how much you want to know. You really want to know why, and it's really hard not knowing.' We have given him the 'standard' adoption responses about Tickle's parents not understanding how to look after him, tried to explain in an age-appropriate way that it wasn't safe for him to remain at home, but the one question that he is desperate for an answer to, I simply don't have one. All I can do is keep repeating 'I don't know why he did it, but it is *definitely* not your fault.'

The police

Up until this point in his life Tickle didn't really know what the police did, apart from 'go nee-naw'. After his disclosures we had been warned that a police officer would want to speak to Tickle, so we had quite a lot of work to do to prepare him. We told him that the police are there to help people who feel worried and sad, and that they are there for when adults make 'bad choices' (a phrase he had picked up from school) in the same way that parents are there for when children make bad choices, to help them stay calm and put things right.

We bought a couple of Playmobil policemen, and I made Tickle a social story using photos of them. If you've not come across social stories before, they are very simple stories, usually illustrated with pictures or photos, used to explain a real-life situation. In this story, there was a little girl (I wanted to keep it slightly removed from Tickle so that it wasn't another trigger for him) who lived with her kind and loving family but had been hurt and frightened by a grown up. The little girl had told her mummy, who had given her a cuddle and called the policeman to come and help. The policeman listened to the little girl and told her she was very brave, then went to see the man who had hurt her, and told him he must not do that any more, and he needed to come with the policeman, who would help him to calm down and not hurt people any more. It's all a little simplistic, but that was the point – I needed something that Tickle could relate to, so we used the same sort of language and actions that we use with him in real life.

Tickle seemed to quite like the story, and he did really well with the real-life policeman too. The real-life policeman was very nice. Softly-spoken, reserved, but happy to get his nice suit down on to our slightly grubby floor and put cars down the slide with Tickle. He asked Tickle a couple of questions like 'How do you spell Tickle' (he had no idea) and 'When is your birthday' (got the month, no idea about the date) as a fairly rudimentary indication of Tickle's level of comprehension. He also asked whether Tickle would like to tell him about the things that happened to him at his other house that had made him feel sad and worried. Much to my astonishment, it seemed that Tickle did want to tell him. He didn't say much, just one brief but illuminating sentence.

Then he curled in on himself, almost like he didn't quite know how to be in his own body. I was grateful I'd taken the time to learn about sensory processing and trauma; I managed to pull Tickle on to my lap and envelope him in a really firm hug, which helped to anchor him and pull him back to normal. The policeman looked Tickle straight in the eye, and said firmly 'That is never going to happen again.' I can't quite remember what happened next, as I was fighting back tears, but I think it was something along the lines of being safe now, he had been very brave, it was a bad thing to happen to him, and so on.

In some ways it was the statement of the police officer that hit home the most for me. It's such a big thing we are trying to deal with. It's such a big thing we have done, in adopting Tickle. He will never have to go through that again.

Assessment and interviews

The next step was for Tickle to be assessed by a police psychologist, called an intermediary, whose job was to decide whether he would be able to give a full interview. What surprised me at the time was how long it took for this to materialise. Husband and I felt like we were right in the thick of things; Tickle had made these huge disclosures, and we were expecting a flurry of activity around us while the Professional People jump to it and Sort Things Out. But that didn't happen, and we had to wait. We were trying to get on with life, but at the same time feeling totally in limbo.

Eventually we did meet the intermediary, who came with two other police officers, and they all tried to squeeze into our tiny house. They played with Tickle, tried to get their recording equipment to work, played some more, played some 'games' designed to test his understanding (which he was quite unimpressed with), and eventually they decided to see if he would talk to them about anything. By this point Tickle was so fed up he had decided he really didn't want to, and did his level best to block them at every turn. Tickle can be pretty stubborn when he doesn't want to talk about something! What I found most difficult was the fact that they didn't want me around while they were talking to Tickle. I can understand why, but looking back now I don't think I would agree to that again. The officers were doing their best to get evidence they could use to arrest Tickle's birth parent, but at that moment in time, was it really the best thing for Tickle?

After they'd been at our house for about four hours and everybody was exhausted they decided to call it a day. However, they asked if I'd bring Tickle in to the station to see whether he would talk in a video suite. I'm not quite sure why they felt he might talk there when he hadn't wanted to talk at home, but they were pretty keen to see if they could get something out of him. It was so hard trying to work out what the right thing to do was; obviously I was really keen for Tickle to talk to the police so we could get some kind of justice for him, but the more I realised what that would entail, and what we'd have to put him through to get that, the more uncomfortable I felt.

A couple of months later, we visited two police officers at a local station, for Tickle to have a go in the interview suite. They took such care of him, which was lovely – let him get in a police van and turn the lights on, made him a special drink, and had loads of toys for him to play with. We'd prepared Tickle as best we could, but the fact was that he had to go in to the video suite with two officers while we waited outside. He did his best, bless him, but he couldn't talk about it. The officers persevered for a while, but it was obvious Tickle was avoiding all their questions.

However, as we were leaving the police station, Tickle suddenly piped up and said 'I was very brave' and then 'That wasn't too bad!'. Husband and I felt hopeful that even though coming to the station hadn't moved the investigation any further forward at least Tickle has some positive associations with the experience of coming to a police station, and in time, might decide for himself that he wants to come back to talk.

The medical

The police also decided they'd like Tickle to have a medical exam. With the benefit of hindsight, there is absolutely no way I would agree to this again; it was invasive and incredibly traumatic for Tickle – and for me as well.

If there had been any chance of getting any results from the exam then it might have been worth it, but all the tests came back clear – which we could have predicted, as by the time he had the examination it was at least two years since any abuse had taken place. We were also asked whether Tickle could go to our GP and have some blood taken, just in case there was anything that might show up – but I put my foot down for that one. Enough is enough.

Moving forward

One thing that's clear is that this is going to be a long, drawn-out process which most likely will not end in a prosecution. I find that hard to swallow some days, knowing that everyone knows what Tickle's birth parent did, but that they are not going to face justice for it.

However, having to endure a court case would be incredibly traumatic for Tickle, and Husband and I (as well as our therapist and the police) simply *have* to concern ourselves with what is best for Tickle, in this moment. It may be that down the line, when he's had a chance to properly process all of this then he can decide for himself that he'd like to take it to trial, but that will be his decision. If we were to go to court at this stage Tickle would need to give a full, videotaped interview, and would have to be examined and cross-examined by barristers in court – either in person or via video link, but still in the court building. To get a conviction, he would have to be absolutely rock solid on his evidence;

the jury would need to be convinced beyond all reasonable doubt. If the barrister asks him 'Are you sure?' And he wavers *at all*, that could be enough for his birth parent to be acquitted. I can't in good conscience put Tickle through that, just because *I* think that his birth parent should be put in prison. It has to be his choice, and I have to manage my own emotions around that.

As I write this, things are on hold. It's not what I had expected, but that is the reality of it. The police are cautious about even bringing Tickle's birth parent in for questioning as they are unlikely to confess, and they are concerned it may aggravate them into trying to find Tickle. The police don't want to do anything that could be risky for us unless they have a very solid case against Tickle's birth parent, which is a decision we support. So Tickle continues with his therapy, and Husband and I try to focus on helping him deal with his trauma day-to-day.

There's not much more I can say in this chapter, except that if this happens to you, you will get through it. I was worried I wouldn't be able to cope, that I wouldn't know what to do, how to be a parent to a child who'd experienced these awful things. I was worried that Tickle might try to act out his abuse, but he hasn't. I was worried that I might traumatise him further by saying the wrong thing, but the worst thing has already happened. As long as I can meet his feelings with empathy, believing him, supporting him, and reassuring him that he is safe in this house, that is all I can really do, for the moment.

It doesn't always feel like enough, but it's all there is.

From the blog

We're having a tough time

Our tough time is continuing. Since Tickle made his disclosures his emotions have been consistently heightened; he's scared of everything, all the time. He'll wake up any time between 3.00am and 5.00am, and will be too scared to stay in his own bed, so either Husband or I will take a duvet and try and kip on his bedroom floor until about 6.00, when we really can't contain him any more. If he wakes earlier he will sometimes go back to sleep (though will wake instantly if we dare to leave the room) but after about 4.30 it's basically a write-off and it's just about keeping him quiet and calm. Sometimes it works, sometimes it doesn't. Sometimes I worry he's going to wake the whole neighbourhood screaming at the top of his lungs.

This is every day, by the way.

Once we give in and let him get up, he's reasonably OK for 45 minutes or so while he's playing and having his breakfast. Sometime towards the end of breakfast the eyes will start to glaze over, the head will tilt to one side, the crazed grin will appear. At this stage, the most important thing is that you spot it early enough so you can grab hold of him before he breaks anything. He then has to be pretty much carried upstairs, and currently it's taking both me and *Husband to wrestle him in to his school clothes. I hold him on my lap, Husband strips and dresses him as quickly as possible, while Tickle screeches and laughs like an escapee from a Victorian lunatic asylum.*

This morning, even though there wasn't any school, the realisation that tomorrow is Monday was enough to have him in tears before he was even out of bed. I managed to contain him enough that he calmed down for breakfast, but by the time Fairy got up he was skirting close to the edge again. After breakfast he followed Fairy upstairs to her bedroom – I'm not quite sure what went on but it culminated in Tickle slamming Fairy's bedroom door so hard that the lock shattered and Fairy was stuck inside.

Husband's lie-in was rudely curtailed as it proved impossible for me to hold both of Tickle's hands and simultaneously break down Fairy's bedroom door. An emergency call was put in to Gran while Husband was busy taking off the door handle and I was so furious with Tickle I didn't trust myself in the same room as him. Desperately needing to do something, *I tried to work out whether I could climb out of the bathroom window and across to Fairy's room, and whether I ought to get dressed first, given that it was pouring with rain. (Tickle in the meantime was repeatedly slamming his own bedroom door.) Husband eventually managed to find a tool on his penknife to slide the bolt across, just as we were discussing the best way to remove the door frame. I bundled Fairy up in my duvet and didn't let go of her for a long time.*

I am finding myself start to doubt whether Tickle is actually in the right place, whether we are enough for him. I am fairly sure if all this had come out while he was in foster care he never would have been considered for adoption at all. I know for a fact that if this had been on his CPR we would have run a mile. But it wasn't, and here we are.

I can't bear the idea of Tickle going back into care, but every time something happens I get more and more frightened, and feel less and less able to cope. If you'd asked me at 9.30 this morning, I would have told you I'd had enough, I can't do this any more. Tickle's behaviour is escalating, and I don't know how far it's going to go.

I don't know how much more of this I can take.

7 Emotion before thought

We're going back into the depths of our brain for this chapter, but first let's recap what we've looked at so far. We've covered a fair bit of theory: in chapter 3 we had an overview of some of the key areas of the brain that are relevant for us as parents of traumatised children. We talked about how responding to a child's needs can shape the way that the brain develops, and how different areas of the brain interact with each other to protect us from (perceived and actual) threat. We also discussed how traumatic memories are stored in the body, and how they can be triggered. In chapter 5 I addressed the issue of attachment, as it is currently such a 'hot topic' in relation to adoption and trauma.

In chapter 4 we looked at strategies for dealing with some of the immediate and challenging behaviours that adopted and fostered children often display. On the whole, these are designed to deal with your current situation, so in this chapter and the next I want to start thinking more long term. To do this, we're going to take a step back and explore the roots of these behaviours in a wider context.

The chapter title, 'emotion before thought' is where we're going to begin with this. 'Emotion before thought' was the core belief of a neuroscientist called Jaak Panksepp who, incidentally, achieved notoriety by demonstrating that rats are ticklish! Panksepp believed that our first response – to everything – is emotional and instinctive, and therefore it's sensible to try and understand our emotional response to something before we analyse our thinking or behaviour.

Emotion

In the course of his work over many decades, Panksepp found seven genetically ingrained emotional systems in our brains, each with its own chemical profile[24]. Panksepp has shown evidence of the seven emotional systems in animal brains as well as human; he believes that they are fundamental systems in the mammalian brain, which as we discussed in chapter 3, has changed very little even with millions of years of evolution. Four systems relate to calm and well-being, and three are 'alarm' systems that trigger high levels of stress hormones.

The well-being systems

The calm and well-being systems are SEEKING, CARE, PLAY, and LUST. (Panksepp used capitals to represent his systems, as an indication of how fundamental they are.) When these systems are activated in the brain they trigger well-being chemicals, and the more a particular system is triggered, the more it will become ingrained as part of our personality[25].

The SEEKING system relates to anticipation, looking for something that is not currently present. It drives an urge for comfort, relationships, to consume, to connect and care for someone, to explore and be curious, for company and companionship.[26] You can easily see the SEEKING system active in young children and babies, from the first instinctive rooting reflex where a baby searches for breastmilk, to the toddler's drive to explore the world and everything in it. In fact, the SEEKING system is essential to survival for young children – they must have a way to get their needs met in order to stay alive. At a more existential level, the SEEKING system drives our desire to learn and grow. However this is also a system that puts us in quite a vulnerable position; you could say that the SEEKING system comes in between the realisation that you have an unmet need, and the comfort of having that need met. For a child who is consistently experiencing their needs *not* being met, they may experience the SEEKING system as unsafe. It makes them vulnerable, it exposes them to the possibility of rejection, again. The same could be said for us as parents of traumatised children – we are seeking love and affection from our children, and an indication that they are beginning to trust us. With repeated rejection (whether actual or perceived), we begin to feel too vulnerable to continue to engage with our child in the same way.

Think back to the most recent interaction you had with your child. Can you identify whether their SEEKING system was active? How did it affect their behaviour? My most recent interaction with Tickle was over FaceTime – he was at Gran's so I could get on with some work, but Gran had called me to tell me Tickle had suddenly gone a bit crazy, running around shouting 'I don't care Gran, I don't care!' The way I interpreted this is that his SEEKING system was wanting to activate but he was feeling too vulnerable to let it. When you're thinking about behaviour in children, asking yourself how the SEEKING system is activated is always a good place to start – it is the 'I have an unfulfilled need' system. In my scenario, Tickle had been at Gran's for most of the day, so it was a reasonable guess that he was missing me. Given his past history, it is also reasonable to assume that the experience of missing your mother (something he experiences daily with his feelings for his birth mother) is extremely upsetting for him, and makes him feel very vulnerable. After speaking with Tickle for a couple of minutes and sympathising with his feelings, I suggested that perhaps he'd like to come home, and he agreed.

The CARE system is our inbuilt propensity to nurture our young. You can see this system in action when young children look after baby dolls, and in ourselves as parents, as we nurture our own children. Every time you sacrifice your own needs for the sake of someone else, your CARE system is active; it allows you to nurture and protect, to tolerate frustration, to enjoy relationships with others, and to give and nourish. Problems with the CARE system can be evident early on, if a child is showing pleasure in hurting children or animals, or otherwise lacking in empathy. The CARE system is the one that relates most closely to attachment, and parents who provide consistent emotional responses can help support the development of their child's CARE system. Unlike attachment, which describes the relationship a child has with his/her caregiver, when we consider Panksepp's emotional systems we can apply these to the way that parents respond to their children, as well as the other way round. If a child's parents have poorly-functioning CARE systems then they are not going to be able to place the needs of their child above their own. They may get frustrated with the child, and resent the demands having a child places on them. The CARE system also requires an element of vulnerability when it is working properly; putting aside your own needs to care for another is not sustainable long-term unless you are receiving *something* back, in other words, you will also be using your SEEKING system alongside it.

Have you witnessed any evidence of an active CARE system in your child? Do they like to look after baby dolls or toys? Perhaps they play with toy food and like to make you cups of tea or bring you things to 'eat'? Can they stroke the family pet, help to clean out their litter or feed them? You might see problems in your child's CARE system if they often hurt others, so it may be useful to try and establish whether this seems to be a deliberate, enjoyable act, or one that stems from fear and the (perceived) need to self-protect. Very recently I've started to notice a huge difference in Tickle's ability to show empathy. I stubbed my toe the other day, and Tickle (unprompted) came to sit by me, saying 'It really hurts when you do that, doesn't it. I did that once and it really hurt.' I also love to watch the way he plays with his toy people, the scenarios he creates with them and how he plays them out. He still needs a lot of input from Husband and myself, modelling caring behaviour, but he has made enormous progress.

The PLAY system is fairly self-explanatory; repeated playful interactions will release well-being chemicals in to the brain, and contribute to the development of a sense of humour and an ability to feel joy. Play is essential to enable a child to grow in to a resilient and resourceful person. I find it fascinating to watch how Tickle's play has developed over time; he's gone from doing a lot of repetitive, soothing play to acting out various scenarios that he's encountered in everyday life, to a lot of 'small world' play, where he has created characters and makes up stories for them.

The fourth well-being system is LUST; it's not one I'm intending to cover in any detail, but as well as lust of a sexual nature it can also refer to the sensual needs that babies are born with, for example needing to be physically close to their mother, breastfeeding, skin on skin contact, etc.

Activating any of the well-being systems will release feel-good chemicals in to our brain such as opioids, oxytocin, and prolactin, sometimes referred to by neuroscientists as 'nature's gift to us'.[27] The chemicals are calming, make us less anxious and less aggressive. The more that these systems are active, the more chemicals that are released, keeping us in a positive state of well-being. Gradually over time, with repeated activation of these systems, this state becomes normal and part of our personality. In other words, if we can help our children establish consistently higher levels of these chemicals in their brain (by activating the well-being systems), then it will shape them in to a calmer, more relaxed version of themselves.

As an adoptive parent I sometimes worry about whether I'm doing 'enough' for Tickle; enough to help him develop, to fill in the gaps in his early development, am I being therapeutic enough, calm enough – the list is endless! I find it reassuring to think in terms of helping Tickle activate and explore these well-being systems; it's something I can do positively and proactively, and even though it doesn't bring instant results I know that I'm building up those calming chemicals in Tickle's brain.

The alarm systems

Stress-inducing parenting will consistently trigger the alarm systems in a child's brain, until – just like with the well-being systems – these heightened and negative emotional states become part of the child's personality.[28] When the alarm systems are activated, the brain releases stress hormones such as cortisol; it's true that *some* level of cortisol can be useful to us, but not when it is delivered in large quantities.

The GRIEF/PANIC system is activated by feelings such as abandonment, or belief that you are going to be abandoned, feeling alone and bereft, or a SEEKING urge that has been rejected.[29] Neglected and abused children can harbour ongoing feelings of insecurity and longing in the GRIEF/PANIC system, as they feel they haven't had anyone who is special to them, and tuned in to their needs. This can sometimes mean lifelong personality problems, and chronic mood disorders such as depression. (It's important here to differentiate between the panic-based fear which is associated with loss and abandonment, and the physical threat of danger that will trigger the FEAR system.)

As parents, it can be useful to reflect on our own emotional systems, and the GRIEF/PANIC system in particular. Have you had any experiences in your life that may have triggered your GRIEF/PANIC system? Was it a one-off, or something more ongoing? I sometimes wonder whether my own grief that came from not being able to have any more children leads me to be seeking something from Tickle that he's not able to provide, a need that it's really not fair of me to ask him to fulfil. There is no easy solution to this, but if I can be aware of what is going on in my own emotional systems it leaves me in a better place to support Tickle in his. For our adopted children, the GRIEF/PANIC system is understandably a very active one. In these situations it's useful for us as parents to consciously think about our CARE system (and making sure that we are in the best emotional place to deal with our children's grief), but also to explore ways that the child's SEEKING system could be activated, as a way of building trust that their needs will be fulfilled.

The FEAR system is activated by scary things in the outside world, and scary sensations coming from within. Frightening (and frightened) behaviour by parents can have a huge negative impact on children's long-term well-being, and research has shown that children who regularly experience frightening parenting (alongside other factors such as failure to repair, lack of parental attunement) are four times as likely to develop a disorganised attachment.[30] Tickle's FEAR system became such an ingrained part of his personality that the professionals working with him in his early life (including social workers and paediatricians) mistakenly believed he would go on to develop a moderate learning disability. Tickle said to me the other day that when his birth parent was hurting him it hurt 'in his brain', so much that he couldn't speak. I think this was his way of telling me that he was so frightened it became completely overwhelming.

The final alarm system is the RAGE system. This system comes from anger at being or feeling thwarted,[31] or feeling out of control. In behaviour terms, this can display as lack of impulse control, violent tendencies, and aggression. Tickle doesn't do RAGE as often as he goes to FEAR or GRIEF/PANIC, but his behaviours have definitely triggered *my* RAGE system on many occasions – that feeling of being totally out of control, trying too hard to help him but being thwarted at every turn. I now know that in that situation I need to leave the room, because oth- erwise I become frightening to Tickle, and his FEAR system will be- come active, leading to escalation for both of us.

Panksepp believes that everyone has the capacity to use all seven systems (including the alarm systems), but the extent to which each system develops is dependent on our life experiences.

Adding in the thought

As I said in the opening of this chapter, Panksepp believed in emotion before thought. These seven systems I have just described are instinctive emotional responses, and Panksepp believed that our feelings and thoughts all stem from there. For example, if our SEEKING system is regularly activated, and we have our needs met, this will lead us to develop empathy, and trust. In psychology this is known as a bottom-up approach; the SEEKING is the starting point, and the rest develops from this point. Equally, if our alarm systems are regularly triggered and our needs are not met then we can develop feelings of shame, anger, blame, and so on. All of these in turn will affect how our higher brain develops; a child who has not had any help with soothing and comforting their alarm systems will not develop the social and emotional intelligence to be able to calm themselves down when under stress. Simply put, the act of comforting a distressed child literally *lays the foundations in the brain* for the child to learn how to comfort themselves.

I believe that taking an overview of these seven emotional systems and their impact on behaviour gives us a more comprehensive understanding of developmental trauma than focusing on a single process like attachment. It has the potential to give us a different perspective on the behaviour of our traumatised children, as well as our own responses to them and their trauma, which if we view as an entire 'eco-system' of parent-child emotional responses, could give us an insight in to the situations we are finding difficult to resolve.

Young children are driven by emotions and impulses. What we as parents are trying to teach our children is how to get 'thought' in between the impulse and the action, or in other words, to enable the higher brain to manage the lower brain reactions. With sensitive parenting, children will grow and learn, and the balance will shift, so that by adulthood, most people will be able to function with conscious thought processes rather than being controlled by impulse. However, without this early input the brain will be lacking vital connections, and problems will occur. In the next chapter we will look at various strategies for supporting your child's brain development with sensitive, responsive parenting.

From the blog

I can sing a rainbow

Little Man and I had a beautiful moment yesterday, on the way back from dropping his sister off at gym. It was a pretty grizzly day round here, wet and soggy most of the day, but by late afternoon the sun was starting to come out, and as we rounded a corner I saw the most enormous rainbow painted right across the sky.

I tried to point it out through the car window, but Tickle had no idea what I was talking about, and kept looking in the wrong direction. We were just about to turn again and lose sight of it, so I made a bit of a flash decision and pulled off the road into a bus stop, and lifted Tickle out of the car so he could have a good look at it.

At first I wasn't even sure if he could see it – he has vision problems and can't see that well even with his glasses – but as I was pointing out the colours I could see, he suddenly said 'Yellow!'

Standing by the side of the road, ignoring the person waiting at the bus stop, we sang the rainbow song. When we got to the last lines, 'I can sing a rainbow…' I stretched out my arm and pointed, tracing the shape of the rainbow with my fingers, and to my delight Tickle copied me.

'What is it?' he asked. (He likes to check these things.)

'It's a rainbow!'

'Why?'

'When it's been raining, and the sun comes out, the sun and rain together makes a rainbow.'

'Oh... my... goodness,' he said.

8 Enabling emotional regulation

In the last chapter we looked at the theory behind our instinctive emotional systems, and how we need to help our children develop their higher brain functions in order to regulate these emotions. In this chapter we're going to look at some different techniques to start teaching this, as well as some more general ideas on creating a nurturing environment that allows your children to grow and learn. If you're reading this as an adoptive parent, you'll already be aware that it's hard work. We are trying to rewire our child's brain.

Fairy is my birth child, and when she was young I taught her how to manage her emotions without even thinking about it; but with Tickle, there's no blank canvas. We are battling against the abuse and neglect, trying to undo six years' worth of brain pathways and reform them in to something that works better for Tickle in this new, safe world he is in. One of the main jobs of the amygdala (meerkat brain) is to work out the emotional meaning of everything that happens to us.[32] If you haven't learned how to use your higher brain to quiet the amygdala's instinctive reactions, then everything will appear as a threat.

Every time you soothe a baby, you are creating pathways in the brain that lead to the ability to regulate emotions. Every time you rock them, every time you kiss them better, console them, meet their needs. Every time you pick up a toddler who has fallen over, clean their scraped knee, fix a broken toy. The path to *self*-regulation of emotions is via *co*-regulation. We need to create those brain pathways first, before the child has access to them on their own[33]. As adoptive parents, we need to be prepared that for some of our children, this will take a Really Long

Time. If you've already been doing this a while, hang in there. You're doing a brilliant job.

The science of comforting

When your child is in a distressed state their body is flooded with adrenaline, and they will be experiencing a variety of symptoms such as increased heart rate, higher blood pressure, tense muscles, and so on. The act of comforting your child brings their body back in to a relaxed state, and the more responsive you are, the greater ability you have to regulate the body's arousal system.

Comforting a distressed child activates their vagus nerve, which originates in the brain stem. The vagus nerve regulates the function of lots of the body's major organs, including the digestive system, heart rate, breathing, and immune system. As you comfort your child, their vagus nerve will restore order to the rest of their body. If you do this consistently over time you can help improve the working of your child's vagus nerve, which in the long term has been linked to effects such as better emotional balance, clear thinking, improved attention, and a more efficient immune system.[34]

The road to regulation

The journey to emotional regulation is a long one, but there are some strategies that you can use in your everyday life to help create that path.

There's a new term I want to introduce here in relation to this: *affect* (pronounced with the stress on the 'a' sound at the start). In psychological terms this describes the external presentation of an emotion – in other words, what you look and sound like when you feel sad, happy, excited, etc. This can be with the tone or intensity of your voice, the expression on your face, how fast or slow you are talking or moving, and so on. When we talk about how to help a child learn to regulate their emotions it's important that we distinguish between the *affect* (the external display) and the *emotion* (felt internally). It is possible to feel an emotion whilst displaying a neutral affect, and it's possible to show a negative affect whilst remaining emotionally neutral.

Babies have very intense emotions, which are often felt and expressed with their whole body. Have you ever seen a crying baby who is completely stiff all over, including all their limbs?! When a baby feels an emotion it is totally overwhelming, so they look to their caregiver to try and understand what is going on. If the caregiver is 'matching' or imitating the infant's emotional affect then the infant is much more able to regulate their emotion.[35] They look at their caregiver and see their own feelings reflected back at them; in terms of Panksepp's emotional states, the infant's SEEKING system is activated (as they have an unmet need) and by reflecting the affect back to the infant, the infant starts to trust that their needs are understood and can be met.

What is really important here is that you match the affect *without* matching the emotional state. For example, when a parent meets their child's anger with anger of their own, things are going to escalate. However, by matching your child's tone of voice, intensity, facial expression, body movement, etc you can send the message that you have understood and acknowledged their emotion. You will then be in a position to introduce some regulation – for example by slowing down your voice, speaking more quietly, or moving less. Matching a child's emotions in this way is much more likely to help them learn to regulate than if you were to stay consistently calm when faced with their emotions. It will bring a feeling of connection, of being 'in this together', and a feeling that the parent has empathised with the child. It's obviously better to meet emotions with calm than with anger, but if a parent stays calm instead of matching a child's own emotional affect, the child is likely to feel less empathy from the parent. The child may even feel that although the adult accepts their emotions, the child is expected to deal with it by themselves.[36]

This general principle of affect-matching can be applied across all ages, and also with learning to manage positive emotions, which can often be almost as overwhelming as negative ones!

Sometimes this ability to 'tune in' to our children's emotions and needs is known as 'attunement'. The good news is that we don't need to be attuned to our children 100 percent of the time (phew!), as the times when we don't immediately respond to their needs can give them a chance to have a go at problem solving for themselves. Some children may find it scary having a parent who is attuned to them, and it may make them feel vulnerable. Tread carefully, but don't let this put you off. Perhaps experiment with different ways of matching your child until you find one that is less threatening to them.

Voicing Feelings

The next natural step from affect matching is to 'voice' what a child is feeling. Adopters may be familiar with this concept already; the idea that you try and put a name to the emotion the child is showing. This helps a child to expand their emotional vocabulary as well as understand what they are feeling; giving a name to the emotion helps to engage the higher brain functions rather than leaving a child overwhelmed within the emotion itself.

Tickle has something of a love-hate relationship with this concept! I wrote in earlier chapters about how he responded positively to it when he first moved in, when he didn't have much emotional vocabulary of his own, but sometimes if I try it now, he will either disagree with me (in a very loud voice!) or he'll just shout 'I KNOW!' I have to confess I am delighted by this, as it means he's recognised his own feelings.

Sometimes he'll even say 'I'm not worried, I'm just cross!' – which is even better!

Tickle's school have also done a lot of work with him on identifying feelings. They have used pictures of faces showing different emotions, and asked Tickle to match up the face to the emotion (starting simply with happy/sad, and progressing on to more complex emotions). They also ask Tickle to match activities to emotions, so for example, does swimming make you happy or sad? Two years of consistent work on this has produced huge rewards; a couple of weeks ago Tickle came in to my bedroom in the morning and told me (in a calm voice) that he was feeling angry because he liked having his favourite teacher in class, and she doesn't work on a Wednesday. I sympathised, and we wrote a message to his teacher in his home-school diary, explaining how he was feeling.

Tickle is a very literal child, with global delay and learning difficulties, and I haven't yet used The Monster as a metaphor with him, as he finds abstract concepts difficult to understand. However on discussion with some adoption friends on Twitter, @adoptionof2 had this to say: 'I used the monster metaphor with [my adopted daughter] to help her define what happens when her mind takes over... [it] separates her behaviour from her. I ask her to see if she can ask him to leave for a bit and join us again when he's left. [It] also lets her feel in control of her feelings as before she was consumed by them'

I really love the way that this child has used the metaphor of The Monster to give her some control over her emotions. By imagining The Monster as a separate entity, she is able to engage her higher brain functions to override the instinctive emotional responses of the amygdala. It also removes any blame from the child herself, and allows her to take control of her behaviour without feeling shame.

Identifying feelings correctly

When Tickle first started therapy, our initial activities were simply about play. Our therapist had a variety of cards with different activities on, and she would ask Tickle to choose one. In one of the sessions, Tickle had chosen an activity that involved Husband and I blowing bubbles towards him. By this time, Tickle was quite good at communicating his feelings to us. When we were just about to blow the bubbles he would laugh and smile, but once the bubbles started would say 'I'm scared'. Husband and I would take him literally, and respond with something like 'It's OK to be scared', but our therapist suggested that Tickle might actually be mis-labelling the feeling. She explained that 'excited' can sometimes feel very similar to scared, and wondered whether Tickle might be confusing the two. We put this to Tickle, and he agreed. Now when he says he's feeling scared, we try to check in with him: 'Do you think that's a scared feeling Tickle, or do you think it might be an excited feeling?'

Setting boundaries and keeping safe

Anger is a tough emotion to live with. Husband and I spent a long time responding to Tickle's anger by trying to calm him down, which seemed perfectly logical to us at the time. However, recently we changed our approach. It occurred to us that, by effectively telling Tickle he wasn't allowed to be cross, we were suppressing his emotion, rather than accepting it and dealing with it. Now, we say is that it is OK to be angry, but it is not OK to hit people. It is OK to be angry, but it is not OK to scream at your sister. (According to my yoga teacher this is a key part of Buddhist philosophy, which is a good sign I think!)

Husband and I are working on helping Tickle separate his emotions from his behaviour, introduce 'thought' between impulse and action, and encourage him to see that he has a choice about the behaviours he chooses to express his emotions. So we might say to him, 'If you want to have a scream, you can can go up to your room to scream. Screaming in here is hurting my ears'. Or, 'If you want to hit something, you can go and hit a pillow. If you hit the table it might break'.

I have to be honest, it doesn't always work(!) and there are times when it seems to create more difficulties than it's solves, but over time Tickle is becoming noticeably more conscious of his actions.

In the long term, Husband and I want to be clear about the boundaries we have put in place in our home – because much as we want to be therapeutic for Tickle, there are three other people living in this house, and we *all* deserve to have a home that feels safe. Our house is *not* a place where intense trauma therapy happens 24 hours a day – though it could very easily become that if we let it. We need to put in the boundaries to create a safe space for all of us.

It was our therapist who first directed us on to this path. She helped us to see that focusing on Tickle all of the time was at the detriment of the rest of our family, and in the long term, this would be to Tickle's detriment too. Our therapist gave us 'permission' to get cross with Tickle sometimes, or to leave the room if he was shouting or screaming at us.

It's OK that Tickle can't always regulate himself, and we accept that sometimes he will behave in a way we don't like, but if it's upsetting me, *it's also OK for me to leave the room.* Yes, it's a separation for Tickle, and it's a temporary disruption to our relationship, but I can repair it once I have had the chance to regulate myself. I was told on a course once that it is a parent's capacity for repair that is the strongest predictor for having a securely attached child[37]. In other words, it doesn't matter if you make mistakes, as long as you can say sorry and make up afterwards.

This approach has been a game-changer for us. We still allow Tickle to feel whatever emotions he feels, and to express them in a way that is safe for him and for everyone else, but our safety is now *as important* as Tickle's. We have to show him that we value our own safety, and that we are able to take charge of that and keep ourselves safe. We have to show Tickle that we can keep ourselves safe *from him* when he is trying to hurt us, without hurting him, and *without controlling him*. We win the argument by bowing out of it.

In this situation, we let Tickle know that we'll be waiting outside, and will pop in occasionally to ask if he wants any help calming down, if he wants a squeeze, cuddle etc. Over time, we have got to the stage where Tickle will recognise that he does need help, even if he's not ready to accept it yet, and sometimes he will even ask for it unprompted.

The results of this have been incredible to watch over the last few months; the couple of little moments where I have seen Tickle stop himself from hitting someone – sometimes me, sometimes other people. On one occasion we were in the park and Tickle was putting his toy down the slide, but a little boy kept picking it up and trying to run off with it. I could see Tickle struggling with himself, but he actually managed to stop himself from hitting the other child, just long enough for me to get to him and envelop him in a squeeze.

Creating a nurturing environment

For children who find direct interventions too much, there is still a lot you can do in your day-to-day lives to support the development of emotional intelligence, and over time you may find they become more receptive to you when they are feeling those extreme emotions. If we think in terms of Panksepp's emotional systems, deliberately triggering the well-being systems can support your child's brain development and complements your responsive work you are already doing with how you react to their alarm systems. Some children who have dealt with trauma by dissociating will need support to be able to tolerate even positive emotions, so developing some strategies for gentle, nurturing play can be really beneficial for them. Ruth Lanius summarises this beautifully: 'in trauma, people just focus on survival and fear. They don't have time to be curious and explore.'[38]

Pets

This is obviously not a decision to take lightly, but having an animal in the home can be a really useful way of helping a child who has never felt safe start to build attachments and recognise positive emotions. We encourage Tickle to help take care of our animals, modelling with him how we feed, clean, and look after something that is dependent on us. We help him to stroke the cats, feel their soft fur, and listen to the sound of them purring. This is a lovely sensory exercise for Tickle, but also can help to ground him in the present, by focusing on things he can see and hear. We teach him to observe how the cats respond to him when he strokes them, how to judge whether they like it or not, when they've had enough. He is learning that the cats are independent creatures, that he can't control what they do or where they go, but that if he is calm and gentle with them they will allow him to stroke and play with them.

Singing

We sing an awful lot at home. When Tickle first moved in, it was the only way we could get through the day. The first car journey home from his foster carers we sang 'This is the way to Mum and Dad's house...' for an hour. The only way to get Tickle to do anything was to sing it. ('Can you put your socks on, socks on, socks on, can you put your socks on, all by yourself...')

Singing is a great bonding activity to do together, and for a child who finds it difficult when you match their affect, singing together may be a way to ease them in to this idea.

Music is an amazing tool that can provide a less threatening way in to a child's emotions. It's soothing, and motivating, and it triggers a deep-down part of your brain that engages your emotion-processing systems[39]. In fact, research has shown that musical games can have a positive effect on prosocial behaviour. In one study where infants were engaged in bouncing games with the researchers, the infants were much more likely to be helpful to the researchers who had synchronised their bouncing with the infants', rather than those who were bouncing out of time with them.[40] The same researchers also later demonstrated that infants who were bounced in sync with an experimenter would also extend this helpfulness to another experimenter who was shown to be friends with the 'in sync' experimenter.[41]

Working at a more conscious level, I sometimes use songs to explore concepts that might be tricky for a child; for example, you can use the song 'If you're happy and you know it' to explore different emotions with children and help them think about appropriate responses to those emotions. By changing the words to 'If you're sad and you know it', 'If you're angry and you know it', etc, it gives you a platform for discussion, or for simply bringing in new ideas. If you're sad and you know it have a cry. Have a cuddle. If you're angry and you know it stamp your feet. Have a squeeze. Throw your ball.

Singing the song (and thereby preparing the strategies) at a time of low stress means that you are doing the groundwork for next time those emotions rise to the surface – you can remind them of the strategies they sang about, and see whether they are able to put any of those in to action. I'm not pretending this is a magic wand, but with repetition and time it will start to bear fruit.

Play to build attachment

I went on a Theraplay course just before we adopted Tickle, and I can thoroughly recommend it. Tickle likes the touchy-feely games, though they won't suit everyone (and do go carefully if your child is resistant to touch, as you may unwittingly trigger a trauma memory). Our absolute favourite is the measuring game, using strawberry laces to 'measure' different bits of your child; their eyebrow, their ear, their arm, their head circumference, their smile, their fingers, anything you can! As well as making the child the focus of your attention, which helps with their self-esteem and self-concept, it has the additional benefits of working on identifying body parts, and you get to eat the laces too!

If your child is amenable to touch you could try some sort of massage, which will trigger well-being chemicals in the brain. Tickle loves me to sing 'Incy-wincy spider' whilst doing various different touches on his back. As the spider climbs up my fingers tickle up his spine, then as the rain comes down I sweep my hands down his back repeatedly. When the sun comes out a gently rub his back in a circular motion (drawing the sun), and then the tickly spider comes back out again to finish.

With young children you can also play clapping games, sitting face-to-face with them and clapping hands together – such as pat-a-cake, or 'A sailor went to sea sea sea'. Alternatively, try sitting your child on your lap for songs such as 'Horsey horsey' (with the jiggling motions), or 'Jelly on a plate'. Both of my children love the 'Jack in the box' game, which involves them jumping high up in the air. This came from a book called *Play Songs* by Sheena Roberts[42], which has lots of excellent suggestions as well as a CD with all the songs on.

Face-to-face games such as putting different coloured stickers on each other's faces are great for developing attachment. Or try peek-a-boo, making noises when your child presses your nose, cheeks, etc. Tickle loves it when I pretend to eat various different body parts and tell him what they taste of – the wackier the better!

It's also worth thinking about games and activities that stimulate the senses. There are endless suggestions for these online, but for starters try games involving water, or sand, coloured shaving foam, different sized stones and pebbles, making a 'sensory walk' where the child walks across various different textures, coloured lights, bubbles, playdoh, and so much more! Try and make use of different body parts, have games that involve crawling on your stomach, standing on one leg, going upside-down or backwards. In addition getting outside in to nature can help calm the body and reduce stress.

Choice

I talked about choice in chapter 4, in the context of dealing with day-to-day challenging behaviours, but it's worth another mention here. When a person experiences trauma, all choice, and therefore control, is lost. When we are able to give our children small choices which they can make themselves to retain an element of control over their environment, we start to stimulate an inner security in them. We are demonstrating that we trust they can make this choice, take control of this situation. We are building their confidence, and their security – in themselves but also within the relationship.[43]

Some children will find it too difficult to make a choice, but I still think it's important to offer it. Tickle initially found choices incredibly difficult, and would get angry with me when I asked him to choose something as simple as what he wanted for dinner. We had to find other ways to introduce the element of choice, for example at bedtime asking him if he wanted to put on his pyjamas first, or do his teeth first.

My best tip for handling choice with a reluctant child is to keep it simple. Offer a choice of two things for them to choose from. If they can't verbalise a choice, maybe have pictures of each thing, one held in each hand. Watch where their eyes go. If they don't point with their fingers, their eyes lingering on one picture may give you a clue about what they are hoping for. If choosing a whole dinner is too hard, break it down: do you want pasta or rice with your dinner? Do you want the red cup or the blue cup? Even when choosing dinner was too much for Tickle, he would still choose which plate he wanted from two that I held out to him.

Children being able to make a choice for themselves is about more than independence; it reaffirms themselves as a human being in their own right who has likes and preferences, and will help to build or reinforce their self-concept, as well as confidence. Choosing which chair they want to sit in, or what they want to watch on TV doesn't sound like much, but it is just one small part of gradually allowing them to find out who they are as a person. Not only that, but by allowing them to make these choices for themselves, we are demonstrating that we trust and value their opinion.

Resources

There are lots of brilliant books for helping children to learn about their emotions. We use the Todd Parr books a lot; Tickle has come to really like *We belong together* which is specifically about adoption. There's also *The Feelings Book*, and *It's OK to be Different* which both children think is brilliant. (Apparently it's OK to eat macaroni cheese in the bath!)

Tickle also likes *William Wobbly*, written by Sarah Naish and Rosie Jeffries. There is a whole series of books featuring Sarah's adopted children, addressing a variety of different issues. For Tickle, *William Wobbly and the Really Bad Day* is the one he most relates to, and the one he keeps coming back to. He's even started to describe himself as having 'wobbly feelings'.

Whatever the issue your child is struggling with, you're likely to find a book that will suit them, somewhere. And if not, then make your own: I have an app called Special Stories, which lets you create your own social stories, upload photos, and record yourself reading each page. We made a story for Tickle about our family, with each of us reading the bits about ourselves, and all of us together at the end saying 'We are a happy family'. He loves it! When I bought it it was priced at £9.99 and it's well worth it; you can export to PDF, iBooks, etc, or just read the stories in the app itself.

Speaking of apps, Sesame Street have an app for emotional regulation called 'Breathe, Think, Do'. It features a monster (which obviously I love) who gets stressed out in a variety of situations, and the game is to help him calm down. It's a very slow-paced app, so it's one to use when you're relaxing, but it's very sweet, and Tickle did learn from it. First you have to help the monster take some deep breaths, then you have to help him think of a solution to his problem; he comes up with three solutions and you pick the one you like the best, which he will then act out.

We bought both children a Worry Eater, which they really like. Fairy didn't let go of hers for about two months, and even Tickle enjoyed telling me what he wanted to write down and let his Worry Eater look after for him.

Regarding worries, we also do a couple of things I mentioned previously – I pretend to take the worries out of Tickle's tummy and put them in my pocket, or he hits the worries out on his pillow. I saw something on the internet the other day which was a toy 'fairy door'; the child puts their hand on to it and it lights up red, which is the fairies 'taking your worry away'. The lights went green when the worry had 'gone'.

The important thing to remember is that we're in this for the long haul. It can feel disheartening when you don't see an immediate response from your child, so make sure you remember to take a step back and reflect on how far you have all come. Now you have some basic knowledge of the developing brain you can feel confident that, regardless of whether you see a response from your child straight away, you are helping to develop the systems in their brain.

From the blog

An amazing thing

An amazing thing just happened.

Tickle and Fairy have had a nice afternoon playing together (mostly – only one incidence of hitting!) and then she decided to read him a story before bedtime.

Next thing I knew she ran out of his room crying; it turns out she had asked to borrow one of his books and he'd not only said no, but pretty much shouted it in her face, repeatedly. Bit of a blow when she'd been sharing her toys and playing with him all afternoon, poor thing.

I went in to talk to Tickle, who was pretty agitated, saying 'My house, my room, my books, I said no!' over and over. He's obviously not ready to share anything, and I told him that's OK.

I also told him that Fairy is upset, not really because of the sharing, but because of the way he refused, shouted at her, etc. We had to go over it quite a lot, with various examples of times when Fairy has shared her toys and how it made Tickle feel, times when someone had shouted and how it made Tickle feel, etc, etc. All this time he was adamant that they were his books and no one else could have them, and equally as adamant that he doesn't like Fairy to be upset and she should basically cheer up.

Eventually, when I have explained about the shouting for approximately the fifteenth time, he suddenly said 'OK, I understand.' Then he said:

'How about this. Tomorrow in the morning we will go on the trampoline together, then go to school, then I will share Fairy my book.'

Jaw on the floor moment. So many little moments, in fact, even before you get to the big moment.

Anyway, we called Fairy up, he announced his plan, they had a hug and now he is asleep. He was pretty concerned that she was still upset, so I explained a couple of times that she was feeling much better now, because he had offered to share and that had made her happy.

'What a kind thing!' he exclaimed, utterly delighted with himself.

9 Other People

I've been really lucky with my friends and family; on the whole they have accepted our decision to adopt, accepted that we have to manage our family in a certain way, and supported us to get on with it. However, sometimes 'Other People' do pop up (for some of my adoptive-parent friends this happens more frequently than others) and try to explain to you that 'all children do that' or 'it's just a phase', or 'you're pandering to them too much'. The thing to bear in mind about other people, is they *don't know*. They think they do, but of course they don't. How could they? This is a chapter for you to photocopy and give to the Other People in your life.

Other People know what it's like to be stressed, to be busy, to have a difficult life. They may be parents themselves. They think they know what it's like to be a stressed parent. Or a stressed working parent. Or a stressed working special needs parent.

What they are failing to understand – I think – is that adoptive parents are already all of those things. We are already working parents, our children have special needs, and we are already trying to balance our own lives, work, extracurricular activities, family commitments, and all of that stuff that comes with a normal, busy life. But *as well* as all that, we are live-in, 24-hour, untrained trauma therapists.

If I were to ask you to go and give an hour's therapy session to a child who had been physically and sexually abused, you would think I was crazy. (Unless you happen to be a clinical psychologist.) You would likely run a mile. You would think 'I can't do that', or even 'I'm not trained for that'.

Then if I said, perhaps, OK it's a two-hour therapy session, actually, and you have to make dinner at the same time, and also make sure your other child is collected from drama club.

Or if I then said, actually – sorry! – this is a 24-hour therapy session, so you will have to put this child to bed as well, this child who has previously been hurt and terrified in a bed, and doesn't really know whether you are one of the adults who hurts children, or even how to tell whether you are. But it's very important that they have a bedtime routine, so during this therapy session you will have to bath them, get them in to pyjamas, and clean their teeth (all in the right order), as well as read them a story. Don't forget you have another child to look after too, who is probably feeling a bit left out at the moment, seeing as this therapy session has been going on all day, but unfortunately, it will probably take a couple of hours to settle this child to sleep first. Oh, and don't forget to have dinner yourself.

Whilst you're doing this therapy session, be mindful of the fact that by putting the child to bed, you are returning them to a place where they have been seriously hurt in the past, so the whole concept of 'bed' may be somewhat triggering for them. Also, you're asking them to go to sleep, but they can only really do that if they feel safe, which, as we have already mentioned, they don't. So when they wake up every two hours during the night ('Oh we have all been there!' the Other People merrily trill!) don't make the mistake of thinking you're off duty, because this is a 24-hour therapy session, remember, so you'll probably have to lie on their bedroom floor for at least 40 minutes while they go back to sleep. And by the time it gets to 5am they probably won't sleep any more anyway.

Speaking of 5.00am, now they are awake, and that means they're scared. Maybe in their first family they didn't always get fed, so that primal brain stem is kicking off, demanding food, NOW, because they are so worried they might not get any. They're not actually hungry, the feeling in their tummy is anxiety, but try explaining that to a screaming 7-year-old. But you're a therapist, remember, so you need to remain calm and reassuring, even at 5.00 in the morning. And don't forget you've got to get the rest of the family up and ready as well, even your other child, who at this point won't leave their bedroom because they are scared of the screaming.

Perhaps, eventually, you manage to get everyone dressed, breakfasted, teeth cleaned, and out of the door with sanity just about intact.

And now you have to go to work.

Because this isn't your job at all. It's your home life.

It's very, very difficult for anyone to understand how pervasive trauma can be in to the life of an adoptive family unless they have experienced it for themselves. What I have described above doesn't happen *every* day in our house, but there was a time when it did. And even when it doesn't, trauma still affects us in dozens of small, medium, and large ways every day.

As I write this, Tickle has been living with us for nearly two years. He still asks me *every day* whether I am going to hurt him. Every. Single. Day.

We can be having the loveliest time, playing together at the park, the two kids scooting home together, hiding from us in the bushes, and then we get home and as I'm turned around taking my shoes off Tickle has hit Fairy for no apparent reason. Simply because he can't handle the emotions he's feeling – even good ones, sometimes.

The harsh reality is that we adopters are not like the 'other' parents. We are unlikely to stand in the school playground chatting about whether our child has reached the blue band in reading yet, or merrily handing out party invitations to the whole class. At the park, we don't casually relax with the other grown-ups while our children play nicely in the distance. It can feel very isolating at times. Adoptive parenting is not normal parenting, and if you're reading this because you're considering adoption, this is a really important truth that you need to understand. It is isolating in so many ways, and it's really important to find your tribe, so you can surround yourself with people who 'get' it. Social media can be great for this – Twitter is a huge source of support for me, and there are also some support groups on Facebook. I have lost count of the number of times that I have seen posts from my friends on social media starting 'I'm just posting this here because you guys are the only ones who will understand...'

Biological children do that too, you know.

If I had to pick one phrase that is guaranteed to trigger my RAGE system, this would be it.

I'm quite sure that this will be meant in the best possible way. My friends are trying to reassure me, in my time of need, that Tickle's behaviour is perfectly normal, and I shouldn't worry. And while I appreciate the sentiment, and while I know that (for him) Tickle's behaviour is, if not normal then at least understandable, this phrase usually makes me want to throw something out of a window.

Other People don't know what it's like, any more than a person who has never had a biological child knows what it's like – until one comes along. And then when you have a child, you reminisce about your pre-child self and laugh at how unprepared you were; all the books, all the antenatal classes, all the web forums and pregnancy clubs – they mean nothing when you actually have another living, breathing human to care for. But once you have a child you miraculously become the font of all knowledge, and you pity the poor pregnant fools who have no idea what they are letting themselves in for.

Until you have another child, then you realise that you had NO CLUE what it was all about, but now you have two, yes, you are the expert.

Until you have a child with Special Needs. Until you have a child with mental health problems. Until you adopt a child. I'm not judging anyone here; it's human nature and I'm guilty of it myself. I was incredibly cocky as a teenager, very confident with myself in my 20s, but as I sail through my 30s and begin to approach the big 4-0 (gulp) I sometimes feel dwarfed by of all the stuff that I *don't* yet know.

Prior to adopting, I was as well prepared as I could be; I have a degree in psychology, and I worked for two and a half years on a research project to do with attachment in new mothers. I have a biological child, so at the time I had eight years of parenting experience, including three years as a single parent. I am a qualified teacher, and I also worked for a year as a mentor for vulnerable children, supporting them in the transition from primary to secondary school. I have worked for the child protection team of my local police as an admin assistant, so I have seen and heard a lot of things from that side too. I have worked for seven years with children with special needs. I have read dozens of books on adoption, on parenting children with trauma, on attachment-focused parenting, brain-based parenting, I went on a course about therapeutic play techniques... I thought I was ready.

I really wasn't ready. I sometimes look back at my pre-adoptive self give a sardonic chuckle when I think how ready and prepared I thought I was. I also sympathise. I can't judge, because how could I ever have known? How could I have known what it would actually be like?

To all parents of biological children, let me say this. You know when your child has a screaming tantrum? When they throw stuff? When it takes three hours to get them to stay in their own bed, and even then they are still shouting and crying? When they stand at the top of the stairs yelling 'I feel like I haven't even got any family!' (I think that was Fairy's version of 'I hate you' – she always was an expressive child!) When they slam doors and stamp their feet, and do the exact thing you've just told them not to do?

Adopted children do that as well.

But with adopted children, there is an additional layer of underlying trauma, uncertainty, panic, woven through their very being, through the fabric of their brain. There is one thing that your biological child will always be sure about – that you are their parent, and you will be there. Regardless of the type of parent you are, they know you will be there. You may shout at them, send them to their room, but you will be there. Children *need* adults in order to survive. Even in extreme cases of child abuse, children are often fiercely loyal to their birth parents, and if given a choice, would choose to go back in to an environment that is physically dangerous to them, just to be with their birth parents.

Imagine your child has been taken from you, possibly in the night, by some adults called social workers (or perhaps the police) who they may have met but don't know that well. They are taken to a new house, to adults they have never seen before, and told they will be living there from now on. Do you think that your child would be fine with this? Or do you think they would be jumping at shadows? Frightened of people? Do you think they might overreact to the tiniest thing? How do you think that they would cope with normal life, after being forcibly taken from you?

For the first five and a half years of his life, Tickle lived in an environment which at times was very frightening and chaotic. He's told us about some of it, and some we have guessed by piecing together little things he says. I'm sure there are things we'll never know. Perhaps every time he heard a raised voice, he was expecting to be hit? Perhaps he expects to be physically punished for making mistakes? For not being quick enough? Perhaps there are certain times of day that he dreads?

Other People don't understand this. Even Tickle's social worker didn't understand this, and really if there is one person you would guess would be on your side in all of this it's your child's social worker. But she'd never lived with a child with a Trauma Monster. So she didn't understand.

Find your tribe. Mine are mostly on Twitter; adoption Twitter is an amazing, supportive community. I'm also blessed to have really supportive friends and family in real life, but I know that's not the case for everyone. So whatever else you do, make sure you find your tribe.

From the blog

Tickle's first Christmas

It's lovely in my house at the moment. We have got decorations up, strings of cards over the mantlepiece to remind us the wider world still exists and hasn't forgotten us, and a massive and ever-growing pile of presents under the tree. Fairy has returned from a couple of days with her dad, and Tickle has been glued to her side ever since. At the moment they are packing bags to go on a pretend holiday, and it's making my tummy go all funny listening to them; Fairy is being the perfect big sister, supporting Tickle in the game and enjoying herself completely, and Tickle is following her round lapping up her every word. Just now Tickle sounded a bit unsure of something, so I called out to let me know if he wanted help, and Fairy comes straight back with 'He's got help Mummy!'

As for me, I'm snuggling up listening to my children play, having sent Husband out for some last-minute shopping, and I thought I'd take a few minutes to write about our preparations for Christmas.

Some things are just as you'd expect: buying presents, opening advent calendars, putting up decorations, stocking up on more boxes of matchmakers than is really sensible. We're having Christmas lunch at my mum's as usual, and my brother and grandpa are coming up as usual. Very normal for us, but completely alien for Tickle. As well as the excitement of Christmas, he has to deal with a huge celebratory lunch, in yet another house, with two people that as of this moment (Christmas Eve) he's never met. So this year Husband and I have been quite consciously adding another layer of preparation in the build-up to the big day.

First, weeks (literally) of agonising over where to have lunch. The main reason we ended up deciding to go to my mums rather than staying at home is that if it all becomes too much for Tickle and we need to escape then we can up and go, without having to interrupt anyone else's lunch. Thankfully Tickle adores Gran and has spent quite a bit of time at her house so it's a nice familiar environment for him. Up until this week he'd never eaten there though, so that was something else we had to think about.

Tickle and I have been 'playing' Christmas morning this week, role-playing what will happen tomorrow, including talking about the order that things are happening in and what we might get in our presents. Tickle has no real clue; most of the things he suggested were foodstuffs (curry, chicken nuggets...), plus a slide and a tunnel. He is oblivious to the pile of presents under the tree, I'm not sure it even occurs to him to wonder what they are, let alone think about whether any of them are for him.

One fairly big issue has been Father Christmas. Tickle knows about him, can tell you what he does (bring presents), where he lives etc, but he is absolutely terrified of the idea of Father Christmas coming in to his room while he's asleep. (I usually avoid going in when he's asleep; I have done it a couple of times and woken him up slightly tucking him in, and he's almost jumped out of his skin.) Tickle and I have come to an agreement that he will put his stocking out on my bed, and I will bring it in to his room once FC has been and filled it up. Bless him.

So, we're nearly there. We have prepared Tickle as best we can, now we just have to wait and see what tomorrow brings.

Only two more jobs remain – wrapping stocking presents, and removing all the bangers from the Christmas crackers.

10 Getting help

One thing that took me completely by surprise when Tickle moved in was how difficult our relationship with social services would turn out to be. At its worst, it was probably more traumatic than our relationship with Tickle.

Initially, social services were very supportive, particularly as we weren't asking for much. I found it difficult to transition from the assessment and matching phase of adoption, where all the focus was on whether Husband and I were 'good enough' to adopt, to the stage where Tickle was living with us and the social workers were expecting us to take the lead in making all the decisions for him. Husband and I felt very naïve, and we put our trust in the social workers, trying to do as they advised, thinking that as the professionals they should know what they were talking about.

When Tickle made his big disclosures, it became suddenly much more obvious that we needed support, and needed it quickly. We had been rushed in to putting in our Adoption Order, so had to ask the court for an adjournment in order to give the Local Authority time to put some support in place. However, although nothing was said directly to us, our social worker grew more worried as she reported to us that Tickle's local authority had 'concerns' over the level of support we were asking for; they seemed to be questioning our commitment to Tickle, whether we were coping – and they even told our social worker that we were refusing to engage with the support that was being offered, which was simply not true.

Only a few months after Tickle's big disclosures we were being repeatedly asked whether we were 'committed' to Tickle. When we asked for help, the response was 'You do realise this is only going to get worse as he gets older?' and 'If you need this much help now, just imagine what it's going to be like when he's a teenager'. We were told that we had unrealistic expectations of Tickle, of the outcomes of the therapy (that they hadn't even identified yet); they acted as if I was asking them to wave a magic wand and make all our problems go away.

If I ever tried to talk to Tickle's social worker about things getting more difficult, her immediate response would be 'Does this mean you're not coping?' 'Do you want me to find another placement for Tickle?'. The trouble was, as social services were failing to properly support us, things became more difficult, we struggled more and more, and Tickle's social worker became more convinced that breakdown was imminent and that she needed to remove Tickle and place him with a family who could cope better. It became such that I no longer felt able to go to her with worries, because I feared she would interpret this as further evidence that we weren't coping.

It would take me an entire book to describe all of the things we went through with social services, and I'm not sure I want to go through it all again anyway, so what I'm going to do is summarise some things I have learnt from this experience.

1. Keep records.

We were having a difficult time trying to get the local authority to submit an application to the Adoption Support Fund. In one meeting we were told definitively that the application wasn't going to be written for another week – this was about five months after our initial professionals' meeting where they had decided to apply. However, I had come to that meeting prepared with a 12-page document outlining concerns that I had with our level of support, all of which were referenced with times and dates that decisions had been made, and evidenced with emails and meeting minutes. About two hours after that meeting had finished I had a call from the meeting chair telling me that the application had gone in for ASF and we would have a decision within a week.

As soon as you start to feel that you are having difficulties getting the support you need, I would recommend keeping records. After every phone conversation, email the person you just spoke to with a summary of the conversation 'just to confirm' your understanding.

2. Confirm actions agreed, and dates for review.

It took me a while to get on top of this, but I would definitely recommend at the end of every meeting asking for an overview of all the actions agreed, who is going to carry each one out, and *when* they are going to be completed. You could also do this by email if you've had a conversation over the phone.

3. You are not 'just' a parent.

Despite the fact that I knew far more about child development than any of our allocated social workers, I frequently suffered from an inferiority complex around them. In Yvonne Newbold's *The Special Parent's Handbook*[44] she recommends dressing for meetings as if you were going to work. It can be a tricky line to walk, but have the confidence to speak out and ask for the support you need. If you've got a friend who is good at being assertive, take them along to meetings with you for support; I took my dad once, who sat there in a suit and essentially chaired the whole meeting. It was incredible, he struck the fear of God in to the hearts of every single person sat around the table. He'd done his research, and he turned up to the meeting with printouts of government guidelines. Watching him ask the virtual school representative to just 'clarify' this point of law and why it hadn't been followed was like a masterclass in how to deal with obstructive professionals.

4. The social workers' job is to support you, and support the placement.

They chose you to be the parents for your child. From that point onward they should be taking their lead from you and supporting you. I did challenge Tickle's social worker over this in one meeting. I said to her that I genuinely didn't know whether her report to the judge was going to say Husband and I were rubbish parents and they thought Tickle should be removed.

Tickle's social worker wouldn't meet my eyes. 'Of course it's not going to say that.'

I was invited to write a letter to the judge, so Husband and I could feel like our voice was being heard in the process. That's all well and good, I said, and I'd be delighted to do so. However, it still doesn't address the fact that we have a team of professionals sat around a table, whose sole purpose for being there is to support us and our child, and I don't even believe that half of you have any confidence in us as his parents. That is an issue.

If I, as Tickle's adoptive mother, am sat here telling you that I don't know whether social services are secretly regretting choosing us for him – that is an issue. If I genuinely think there is a chance that social services are not correctly representing us to the judge – that is an issue.

5. Keep your child at the centre of discussions

It sounds silly, I know, but you would be amazed at how easily discussions that *were* about your child morph in to discussions about how there is no budget for the things you are asking for. Our (excellent) social worker had a great turn of phrase for this – support should be 'needs led', not 'resource led'. In other words, you should arrange the support package by choosing services that best meets the child's needs, rather than going with whatever you happen to have available and hoping that will work.

Yvonne Newbold suggests taking a framed photo of your child and putting it on the desk at the meeting. I have done this and found it really helped bring Tickle in to the room. I'm not sure whether it made a difference to the outcome of the meeting, but it helped how I felt about it.

6. You will need some sort of therapy

It may not necessarily need to happen right at the start of the placement, but I don't know of any adoptive family that hasn't needed *some* form of therapy, somewhere along the line. It is worth having the discussions early on in placement, and if you can, getting an agreement about support in your adoption support plan. Finding the right therapy is absolutely priceless, and worth all the effort it can take to get it.

I want to round up this section by acknowledging that there are some amazing social workers who are doing excellent work for adoptive families, and in fact we had a lot of support from our (voluntary) adoption agency, both from our allocated social worker and various other members of the team. However, our struggle with the local authority is a very common story which is frequently echoed by my friends on adoption Twitter. I wish it wasn't, but that appears to be the way of things at the moment, so it's as well to be prepared.

From the blog

And finally

Fairy and I went for a walk to the park this evening. We have decided it's going to be our evening ritual; Tickle goes to bed and we go out for a walk, a bit of fresh air, and to get the step count up on our Fitbits (Fairy has managed to snaffle Gran's old one and is now obsessively tracking everything).

As we were walking I asked how she was feeling about things at home at the moment..

'I decided something yesterday.' she says. 'I have had enough of The Monster.'

'OK.'

'But the quickest way to get rid of The Monster would also get rid of Tickle, and I don't want to do that.'

We walked some more. We played at the park. I went on the zip wire, which she thought was hilarious. We walked home the long way; it was about 8.45pm and she brought the subject up again.

'I have had enough of The Monster, but the quickest way to get rid of it would also get rid of Tickle, and I don't want to do that.'

'I don't either.' I said. 'What do you think we should do?'

'I think we should keep trying.' she said.

So that's what we'll do.

Epilogue

One year later

For one reason and another, this book sat around on my computer for quite some time after I'd finished writing it. A year down the line and about to publish, I've been going through the book for the final proofing and – realising how much has changed – I thought it would be nice to write a final chapter to let you know how we're doing.

As I write this, it's only a few days before Tickle's ninth birthday, and it's a complete contrast to the first one that he spent with us. I still remember three years ago trying to take a screaming Tickle in to the toy shop to choose a birthday present. I remember on the day itself, Tickle sitting surrounded by piles of wrapped up presents and asking what he was supposed to do with them. I remember him seeing the cake in the shape of Thomas the Tank Engine, and not understanding that it was a cake.

This year, however, Tickle has been planning his birthday for quite some time. He has requested a cake in the shape of a slide, and has told us he wants another baby doll for his birthday present, and that he's going to call it Bailey. (This will bring his total of baby dolls to four, as Bailey joins his adopted brothers Kando and Leo, and his adopted sister Sienna.) Tickle also wants a buggy for Bailey, and somewhere for him to sleep, and some pyjamas, and some ear defenders, because apparently babies don't like loud noises. He has very helpfully told us what colour each doll likes (Bailey likes black, Sienna likes green, Leo likes blue, and Kando likes pink), so we know what colour the pyjamas and ear defenders should be. He still likes cars, he tells me, but he thinks he's got plenty of them by now. Tickle has also requested a birthday party (his first ever, we think) and he's been able to identify half a dozen children from school who he wants to invite, and quite a few that he doesn't!

We are in the midst of the pre-Christmas craziness at the moment, and as usual the 'loopy' or dissociated states have got more frequent. They often happen at dinner or bedtime, or when we get back home from being out somewhere, but it's been a good few months since we've had a meltdown when we're out and about. We're coping with the meltdowns much better as well; I try to think of them as a signal that Tickle is feeling vulnerable, and that I need to up my nurture quotient. If it happens during a mealtime, we will often feed Tickle as if he were a baby, sometimes with him sat on one of our laps. Husband plays the game where you make aeroplane noises with the spoon, but I am not as good at the noises so I tend to sing songs about whatever Tickle is eating. We empathise a *lot* – 'Gosh, Tickle must have some *really* big feelings! Isn't it *so* hard to eat your dinner when you've got such big feelings!' – and I try to match my tone of voice to his, to reinforce the idea that I am fully understanding what he is communicating to me. I'd say about 80 per-cent of the time Husband and I can now de-escalate a meltdown fairly quickly, and without either of us getting too wound up by it. Obviously there are still days when Tickle tries to flush his flannel down the toilet or throw toys out of the window, but they are the exception rather than the rule.

One thing I am really pleased to report is that child-to-parent violence is now very rare, and when it does occur it is not nearly as prolonged or as frenzied as it was. I think it's been almost a year since I last felt actually unsafe because of Tickle's actions, which, when I think about how I was feeling when I wrote some of the earlier blog posts in this book, is nothing short of miraculous. Unfortunately, the CPV does seem to have transferred to school and become child-to-teacher violence with a couple of Tickle's favourite staff members. Thankfully his school is brilliant; we are doing our best to support Tickle's teacher, and school have been able to access some training on adoption and trauma via our therapist, as well as some input from an educational psychologist who specialises in traumatised children.

I suppose the real testament to how far we've come is that in our most recent therapy session, our therapist told us she doesn't think we need to keep seeing her. I have to confess my instant response was one of panic, but she's right – we're doing OK. Tickle himself hasn't really been able to access the therapy yet; he gave it a try, but it was clear that he wasn't ready to talk in that setting. Our therapist says we will be able to refer ourselves back in to their service whenever we feel we need to, so if Tickle does want to talk about things at any point we still have that option. I'm quite surprised in myself that I can feel confident about signing off from therapy even though Tickle hasn't been able to access it. When we first starting seeing our therapist I so badly wanted Tickle to talk to someone, and to deal with all his wobbly feelings, but I feel much less attached to that as an outcome now. I don't feel so desperately in need of a short-term 'fix' for Tickle's behaviour, because I feel stronger in myself, and more confident that the way we parent Tickle therapeutically will pay off in the long term.

As Tickle calms down, other parts of his personality have begun to shine through. He is a really caring and empathetic child and loves to do nice things for other people. He is really getting a good grasp on how to manage his own emotions and is almost always able to say if he needs a cuddle or a squeeze when prompted, and sometimes even spontaneously.

Recently, one of our cats had to be put down and our whole family was devastated. Husband and I were quite worried about how Tickle would react – I was expecting mega-meltdowns, dissociation, screaming, the works, but Tickle really surprised me. He snuggled with me in bed, saying 'I'm sad, I didn't want Etta to die, please can Etta not die?' He asked me why I was crying, and when I said I was sad about Etta, he said 'I'm sad too, I'm crying too, I don't want Etta to die.' He wasn't actually crying, but he was pretending to, and I have no doubt he was feeling the emotions. We sat there for at least half an hour, crying together, feeling sad. Even as I write this, I am stunned at how well Tickle was able to sit with such an intense negative emotion that day, particularly when I was so incapacitated by it. In actual fact, I think it was *because* I was so obviously sad that Tickle was able to recognise his emotions in me, and use them to help him understand what he was feeling. Later on after he'd gone off to play he popped back in to see me and asked why I was still crying. When I told him I was still sad about Etta, he sympathised, and offered to get me something to eat or drink to help me feel better! Things like this really give me faith that change is possible for Tickle, and that even though it doesn't feel like it when we are in the thick of things, we are making a tangible difference.

Tickle is developing cognitively as well. Reading is still a challenge, and he still only recognises half a dozen letters, but he is able to symbol-read quite well, which gives him a bit of independence. He has a symbol timetable made up for him every day by his teacher, so when he comes home from school he's able to tell me what he'll be doing the next day, and which teacher he's with. Maths is another story altogether; Tickle's counting has come on in leaps and bounds, and he has even progressed to some basic adding up and subtracting, some of which he can do in his head without concrete objects present. For a child who was expected to have a moderate learning disability that is really astonishing progress, and I am so proud of him. I don't spend a lot of time thinking about the future, but little things like this give me hope that Tickle might be able to have a degree of independence when he's older.

Tickle loves to sing. I mentioned earlier in the book that we had to sing *all* the time when Tickle first moved in – we don't have to any more, but we still do it a lot! Tickle has developed a habit of noticing things in his environment and relating them to songs he knows, so if we're walking along and notice a Christmas tree decorated with lights, we have to give it a couple of rounds of 'We wish you a merry Christmas' before we can walk any further. Likewise with horses and 'Horsey horsey don't you stop'!

When I think about the things that have helped us over the last couple of years, virtually all of them fall in the category of 'look after yourself first'. *Self-care is not optional!* It may mean making a significant mental shift, thinking about putting yourself first occasionally, but it is worth it – for you, and for the rest of your family.

This might sound like a strange thing to class as self-care, but Husband has been off work for over a year now. We were lucky (or forward-thinking!) in that we'd set up a life assurance policy a couple of years previously, which covered Husband if he were to be signed off work through illness, including stress. Obviously I wish it hadn't had to come to that, but taking an action to *stop* doing things can sometimes be the most positive thing you can do. Husband has been able to take more care of himself without the additional stress of working full time, and having one of us at home all day is making a huge difference to family life – it won't be possible for everyone, I know, but take whatever help you can, wherever you can get it! Tickle has now managed three sleepovers at Gran's house, and we have arranged for a family friend to take him out for a morning about every three to four weeks. These little pockets of calm make such a difference, and we don't feel the slightest bit guilty about spending the whole morning in bed watching reruns of *Buffy the Vampire Slayer*.

As for the rest of us, we're still trundling along. Life is still challenging; Fairy has recently been diagnosed with autism, and we suspect she has ADHD as well. She's been struggling with school for a while now, so we've decided to withdraw her for the foreseeable future and see if home education works for us. I am exploring my own neurodiversity, which has been an interesting journey to say the least. But the important thing is, we are actually doing OK. Not brilliantly, but OK. And after all we've been through these last few years, I think I'll take that.

To my readers: Thank you for reading Me, the Boy, and The Monster*! It has been a real labour of love and I'm so excited that I'm finally able to share it with you, I am pretty much dancing on the table. I really hope that if you've managed to get this far through it then you've got something useful out of it! I'd love to hear from you if you've got any comments on the book, questions, suggestions of things you'd like to hear more about, or stories from your own families.*

You can visit my website at http://catmcgill.uk or contact me on Twitter @folkycat.

I'd love to hear what you thought of the book, so please leave me a review on Amazon!

If you'd like to read more about my family, and be the first to hear exciting news and updates on my work then why not take advantage of this offer for the MTBTM Readers' Club!

Readers' Club Offer!

A special offer to all readers of 'Me, the Boy, and The Monster'!

If you've enjoyed reading about our family you might like *What's Next for Unicorns?* – a lighthearted and often laugh-out-loud foray in to the developing brain of our little Fairy as she learns to talk. Available for FREE when you sign up to Cat's mailing list.

To claim your FREE ebook visit http://catmcgill.uk/wnfu

I'D LIKE TO THANK MY amazing family; my Husband, my anchor. I couldn't do any of this without you. Fairy, you beautiful soul. You are such a special person. Tickle, you amaze me every day with your resilience and your strength. I love you all so much.

Thank you to my parents and step mum for their emotional and practical support, and for accepting Tickle despite the havoc (and physical injuries) he has wreaked on us all. Thank you for seeing past The Monster, and loving the boy.

I'd like to thank everyone who read and proofed early versions of the book for me, especially my editor Hannah (@HLMeadows), and Courtney (@chemcoco) who proofed the book from the point of view of an adult adoptee.

To my friends: there are no words to describe how humbled I feel at the incredible support we have been shown throughout all of this – the food parcels, chocolate-by-post, virtual and real hugs, and the acceptance that you couldn't possibly understand what we were going through, but you were there for us anyway. I am proud and grateful to have such wonderful people in my life.

To my Twitter family: you're the best. #glowmo

For more information about me and my work visit http://catmcgill.uk.

ENDNOTES

[1] 'On Being' interview 9 March 2017 retrieved from http://onbeing.org/programs/bessel-van-der-kolk-how-trauma-lodges-in-the-body/ on 14 March 2017.

[2] 'How to work with Trauma that's trapped in the Nervous System'. Part of the National Institute for the Clinical Application of Behavioural Medicine's 'Treating Trauma' Master Series. http://www.nicabm.com/

[3] Donovan, S. (2015). *The Unofficial Guide to Adoptive Parenting: The Small Stuff, The Big Stuff, and The Stuff In Between*. London: Jessica Kingsley Publishers.

[4] Omer, H. (2004). *Non-Violent Resistance: A New Approach to Violent and Self-destructive Children*. Cambridge University Press.

[5] Panksepp, J., Texas, et al (2012). *The archaeology of mind: neuroevolutionary origins of human emotion*. New York: WW Norton & Co. Cited in Sunderland, Margot (2016). *What Every Parent Needs to Know. Love, nurture and play with your child*. London: Dorling Kindersley Limited

[6] Evans, Jane (2015). 'Taming and Tending Your Meerkat Brain', a talk given at TEDxBristol. Recording retrieved from https://www.youtube.com/watch?v=qKlzd-H2X9w on 6 December 2018.

[7] MacLean, P. (1990). *The Triune Brain in Evolution*. Cited in Kazlev, M. Alan; et al. (2003-10-19). "The Triune Brain". KHEPER. Retrieved on 28 December 2017.

[8] Sunderland, Margot (2016). *What Every Parent Needs to Know. Love, nurture and play with your child.* London: Dorling Kindersley Limited.

[9] Sunderland, Margot (2016). *What Every Parent Needs to Know. Love, nurture and play with your child.* London: Dorling Kindersley Limited.

[10] Sunderland, Margot (2016). *What Every Parent Needs to Know. Love, nurture and play with your child.* London: Dorling Kindersley Limited.

[11] How to work with Trauma that's trapped in the Nervous System" Part of the National Institute for the Clinical Application of Behavioural Medicine's 'Treating Trauma' Master Series. http://www.nicabm.com/

[12] Levine, P. 'How to Work with Emotional and Procedural Memory in the Case of Preverbal Trauma'. Part of the National Institute for the Clinical Application of Behavioural Medicine's 'Treating Trauma' Master Series. http://www.nicabm.com/

[13] Brewin, C.R., Dalgleish, R., & Joseph, S. (1996). 'A dual representation theory of posttraumatic stress disorder'. *Psychological Review, 117(1),* 210–232. Cited to author as part of course for parents of children who have been abused.

[14] Hughes, Daniel A. (2009). *Attachment-focused parenting: effective strategies to care for children.* New York: WW Norton & Company Inc. p 69.

[15] Bowlby J. (1969). *Attachment. Attachment and loss: Vol. 1. Loss.* New York: Basic Books. Cited in McLeod, S. A. (2009). *Attachment*

Theory. Retrieved from http://www.simplypsychology.org/attachment.html on 2 April 2018.

[16] McLeod, S.A. (2018). *Mary Ainsworth*. Retrieved from https://www.simplypsychology.org/mary-ainsworth.html on 6 December 2018.

[17] Siegel, D., and Sroufe, A. (2011) .*The Verdict is In*. Retrieved from https://www.drdansiegel.com/uploads/1271-the-verdict-is-in.pdf on 6 December 2018.

[18] 'How to work with Trauma that's trapped in the Nervous System' http://www.nicabm.com/treatingtrauma2017/confirmed-3/ retrieved on 3 October 2017.

[19] Burgo, Joseph (2013). 'The Difference Between Guilt and Shame'. *Psychology Today*, retrieved from https://www.psychologytoday.com/us/blog/shame/201305/the-difference-between-guilt-and-shame on 2/4/18.

[20] Kohlberg, L. (1958). 'The Development of Modes of Thinking and Choices in Years 10 to 16'.PhD. Dissertation, University of Chicago. Cited in McLeod, S.A. (2013). Kohlberg. Retrieved from http://www.simplypsychology.org/kohlberg.html on 2 April 2018

[21] Hughes, Daniel A .(2009). *Attachment-focused parenting: effective strategies to care for children*. New York: WW Norton & Company Inc., p164.

[22] McLeod, S.A. (2008). 'Self concept'. Retrieved from http://www.simplypsychology.org/self-concept.html[1] on 2 April 2018

1. http://www.simplypsychology.org/self-concept.html

[23] Piaget, J., & Cook, M.T. (1952).*The origins of intelligence in children*. New York, NY: International University Press. Cited in McLeod, S.A. (2015). *Jean Piaget (schema theory).* Retrieved from http://www.simplypsychology.org/piaget.html on 2 April 2018.

[24] Panksepp, J., Texas al (2012). *The archeology of mind: neuroevolutionary origins of human emotion*. New York: WW Norton & Co. Cited in Sunderland, Margot (2016). *What Every Parent Needs to Know. Love, nurture and play with your child*. London: Dorling Kindersley Limited

[25] Perry, B.D., et al (1995). 'Childhood trauma; the neurobiology of adaptation and use-dependent development of the brain: how states become traits'. *Infant Mental Health Journal*, 16: 271-91. Cited in Sunderland, Margot (2016). *What Every Parent Needs to Know. Love, nurture and play with your child*. London: Dorling Kindersley Limited.

[26] Tucker, Joanna (2018). 'Panksepp and Biven's 7 primary process emotional systems, and how they inform our understanding and practice'. Presentation as part of a course run by OXPIP, 22 Jan 2018.

[27] Panksepp, J., Texas al (2012). *The archeology of mind: neuroevolutionary origins of human emotion*. New York: WW Norton & Co. Cited in Sunderland, Margot (2016). *What Every Parent Needs to Know. Love, nurture and play with your child*. London: Dorling Kindersley Limited

[28] Sunderland, Margot (2016). *What Every Parent Needs to Know. Love, nurture and play with your child*. London: Dorling Kindersley Limited.

[29] Tucker, Joanna (2018). 'Panksepp and Biven's 7 primary process emotional systems, and how they inform our understanding and practice'. Presentation as part of a course run by OXPIP, 22 Jan 2018.

[30] Madigan S., Bakermans-Kranenburg M., Van IJzendoorn M., Moran G, Pederson, Benoit D. (2006) 'Unresolved states of mind, anomalous parental behavior, and disorganized attachment: A review and meta- analysis of a transmission gap'. *Attachment & Human Development*. 2006; 8:89–111. Cited in Beebe et al (2012). 'On the Origins of Disorganized Attachment and Internal Working Models: Paper I. A Dyadic Systems Approach.' *Psychoanal Dialogues*. 2012; 22(2): 253–272. Retrieved from https://www.ncbi.nlm.nih.gov/pmc/articles/PMC4225631/pdf/nihms-561443.pdf on 8 April 2018.

[31] Tucker, Joanna (2018). 'Panksepp and Biven's 7 primary process emotional systems, and how they inform our understanding and practice'. Presentation as part of a course run by OXPIP, 22 January 2018.

[32] Sunderland, Margot (2016). *What Every Parent Needs to Know. Love, nurture and play with your child*. London: Dorling Kindersley Limited.

[33] Sunderland, Margot (2016). *What Every Parent Needs to Know. Love, nurture and play with your child*. London: Dorling Kindersley Limited.

[34] Sunderland, Margot (2016). *What Every Parent Needs to Know. Love, nurture and play with your child*. London: Dorling Kindersley Limited.

[35] Hughes, D., & Baylin, J. (2012). *Brain-Based Parenting: The neuroscience of caregiving for healthy attachment*. New York: WW Norton & Company.

[36] Hughes, D., & Baylin, J. (2012) .*Brain-Based Parenting: The neuroscience of caregiving for healthy attachment*. New York: WW Norton & Company.

[37] Tucker, Joanna (2018). 'Panksepp and Biven's 7 primary process emotional systems, and how they inform our understanding and practice'. Presentation as part of a course run by OXPIP, 22 January 2018.

[38] Lanius, R. In 'The Neurobiology of Attachment.' Part of the National Institute for the Clinical Application of Behavioural Medicine's 'Treating Trauma' Master Series. http://www.nicabm.com/

[39] Cirelli, L., et al (2014). 'Interpersonal synchrony increases pre-social behaviour in infants'. *Developmental Science*, Volume 17(6), 1003-1011. Cited in Sunderland, Margot (2016). *What Every Parent Needs to Know. Love, nurture and play with your child*. London: Dorling Kindersley Limited.

[40] Cirelli, L., et al (2014). 'Interpersonal synchrony increases pre-social behaviour in infants'. *Developmental Science*, Volume 17(6), 1003–1011.

[41] Cirelli, L., et al (2016). 'Social Effects of Movement Synchrony: Increased Infant Helpfulness on Transfers to Affiliates of Synchronously Moving Partners'. *Infancy*, 21(6), 807–821.

[42] Roberts, Sheena (2000). *Play Songs: Action Songs and Rhymes for Babies and Toddlers*.

[43] Ogden, P. In 'The Neurobiology of Attachment'. Part of the National Institute for the Clinical Application of Behavioural Medicine's 'Treating Trauma' Master Series. http://www.nicabm.com/

[44] Newbold, Yvonne (2014). *The Special Parent's Handbook*. UK: Amity House.

About the Author

Hello! Thanks for reading my book :) I'm Cat, I'm a musician and writer, and a mum to two children with Special Needs. I'm autistic myself as well, though I wasn't diagnosed until my late thirties. Ever since I can remember I've been fascinated by people - their relationships with one another, what makes them tick, how they learn, etc. I decided when I was nine that I was going to study psychology at university, and - never having been able to make my mind up whether I wanted to be a musician or a psychologist - I have bounced between the two ever since.

My debut book is called 'Me, the Boy, and The Monster', and is an honest account of the first couple of years with our adopted son, and the trauma he faced, and still faces. I've tried to pull together a few of the psychological theories that have really helped me to understand Tickle's behaviour, and explain them in an accessible way, giving examples from our day to day life.

As I write this I'm about to undertake a project called 'Adopting a Musical Approach' where I'm looking at how I can use music to support adopted children and their families. For more information do have a look at my website, or say hi on social media - you can find me @folkycat on Twitter, Facebook, and YouTube.

Read more at www.catmcgill.uk.

Printed in Great Britain
by Amazon

48828019R00118